RAIL CENTRES:
NOTTINGHAM

Front cover, top:
'D3' 4-4-0, No 4307 with the Derby-Grantham working at Nottingham
Victoria on 30 August 1939. *J. F. Henton*

Front cover, bottom
The modern face of Midland station: a Class 158 heads west past the site of
the former MR goods yard with a working for Birmingham New Street.
Author

Back cover, top
On 30 March 1965, the Midland Pullman leaves London Road carriage
sidings. *J. F. Henton*

Back cover, bottom
4-4-0, No 41063 passes Long Eaton Junction on 15 March 1952 with the
Nottingham-Sheffield slow train. *J. F. Henton*

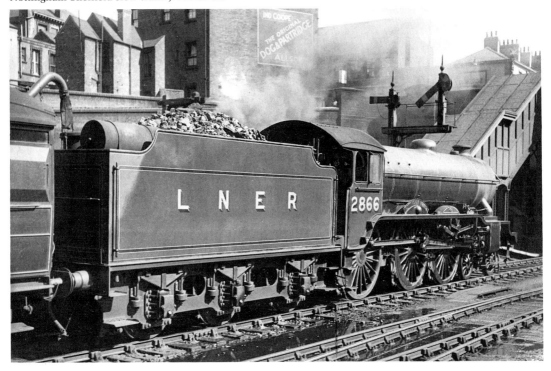

Above:
Named after the city's 'premier' football team, LNER 'B17' 4-6-0 No 2866
Nottingham Forest was photographed on 3 June 1939 at Nottingham
Victoria heading the 2.20pm from Manchester. In front of the locomotive is
the station exit to Parliament Street abandoned in the 1960s.
T. G. Hepburn/Rail Archive Stephenson

Above right:
08.45 on Saturday 6 March 1993: No 47276 stands in one of the centre
roads at the south end of Nottingham station as No 158849 arrives exactly
on time having left Norwich at 05.52 on its journey to Liverpool (due
11.29). On the left the 09.00 (SO) HST is shortly to depart for London
St Pancras. *Author*

Front end paper:
Ex-GN 4-4-2 No 4420 pulls away from Nottingham Victoria past the South
signalbox with the 3.25pm slow Sunday train to Rugby on 7 May 1939.
J. Cupit

Back end paper.
Type 4 No 44 *Royal Irish Fusilier* heads south over the River Trent with an
up mineral train from Toton yard in the mid-1950s.
T. G. Hepburn/Rail Archive Stephenson

RAIL CENTRES:
NOTTINGHAM

MICHAEL A. VANNS

IAN ALLAN
Publishing

Contents

First published 1993

ISBN 0 7110 2170 8

© Ian Allan Ltd 1993

Published by Ian Allan Ltd,
Shepperton, Surrey; and
printed in Great Britain by Ian
Allan Printing Ltd,
Coombelands House,
Addlestone, Surrey KT15 1HY.

Abbreviations

Acknowledgements

Wherever possible contemporary sources have been consulted during the writing of this book, and a fully referenced text of this work is available for consultation in the Nottinghamshire County Council's Local Studies Library and the Nottinghamshire Archives Office, Nottingham.

I would particularly like to thank the following individuals and organisations who helped me during the research for this book: all the staff who had to retrieve the numerous and unwieldy railway company official deposited plans in the Nottinghamshire Archives Office for me; all those who helped in the Nottinghamshire County Council's Local Studies Library, especially Mrs Dorothy Ritchie when it came to choosing photographs; the staff of the National Railway Museum's library, and, as a native of Nottingham, I hope that Mr Philip Atkins feels the effort was worthwhile; Mr Lewis in the Geography Department, Nottingham University; Mr Brian Carter of the Public Record Office, Kew; Mr John Dawson of Regional Railways' PR Department for allowing me access to the former LMR library in Birmingham; Mr David McIntosh, District Manager of Regional Railways East Midlands & Lincolnshire District, for granting me an interview; Mr John Edgington for reading through the final chapters; I am most sincerely grateful to Mr Brian Stephenson for the time spent choosing and then printing up photographs for this book; and for providing access to the Ian Allan Library, and accommodation on my visits, my thanks go to Mr Peter Waller.

Finally, this work would have been incomplete without the contribution of the following people and organisations, and my apologies for any omissions: Mr John Henton; Mr Don Powell; Mr John Marshall; Mr J. Cupit; Mr J. P. Wilson; Mr D. Thompson (via Robert Humm & Co); Mr R. J. Essery; Mr Roy Anderson; Mrs Sentance; Leicestershire County Museums, Art Galleries & Record Service; *Nottingham Evening Post*; Hulton Deutsch Collection Ltd; The Butterley Photo Archive; Cambridge University Collection of Air Photographs; Ironbridge Gorge Museum Trust; The Erewash Valley Museum; Mr David Houston and Mr Ian Brown for carefully printing many of the photographs reproduced in the book; mum and dad.

Michael A. Vanns
Coalbrookdale
Spring 1993

LNWR	London & North Western Railway		MX	Mondays excepted
LNR	London Northern Railway		NAO	Nottinghamshire Archive Office
LPC	Locomotive Publishing Co		NCB	National Coal Board
LT&S	London, Tilbury & Southend Railway		NCCLSL	Nottinghamshire County Council Local Studies Library
M&GN	Midland & Great Northern Joint Railway		NHFU	Nottingham Historic Film Unit
MCR	Midland Counties Railway		NMR	North Midland Railway
MGJR	Midland Grand Junction Railway		PSO	Public Service Obligation
MO	Mondays only		RCTS	Railway Correspondence & Travel Society
MOD	Ministry of Defence		S&T	Signal & Telegraph
MPD	motive power depot		SLS	Stephenson Locomotive Society
MS&L	Manchester, Sheffield & Lincolnshire Railway		SO	Saturdays only
MR	Midland Railway		SR	Southern Railway
MS&L	Manchester, Sheffield & Lincolnshire Railway		SX	Saturdays excepted
			Th/SX	Thursdays & Saturdays excepted
			UDM	Union of Democratic Mineworkers

Introduction

The spine of Nottinghamshire is made up of Bunter Sandstone extending through the county from north to south, with the 'exposed' coalfield to the west and the 'concealed' coalfield to the east. Nottingham lies on the southernmost tip of this sandstone where the River Trent flowing southwest to northeast, along with its flood plain, gave the early settlement its southern boundary. The Normans built their castle on the most prominent part of the sandstone ridge and, immediately to the east, a large open market-place soon developed establishing the town's role as a trading centre with all the attendant services and professions. As Nottingham also lay at a point beyond which the Trent was not easily navigable from the Humber estuary, it took on the role of an inland port and this, combined with a mediæval bridge across the river, confirmed the town's trading importance. Nottingham prospered and Defoe in his travels described the town as '...one of the most pleasant and beautiful in England'.

The River Trent and Canals

All manner of goods travelled along the River Trent, but by the beginning of the 19th century the most important cargo transported down the river to Nottingham, Newark, Gainsborough and on to the Humber was coal mined along the Nottinghamshire/Derbyshire border. It reached the river at Sawley via the Erewash Canal, completed in 1779, and three vital feeder waterways: the Cromford Canal opened in 1790; the Nutbrook Canal finished three years later; and the Nottingham Canal reaching Nottingham via Trowell, Wollaton and Lenton in 1796. In 1783 an Act of Parliament created the Trent Navigation Co with powers to improve the river to allow the passage of boats carrying 30-40 tons of goods and William Jessop the company's engineer made his home at Newark. Ten years later work started on a canal between Nottingham and Grantham and, when this opened in 1797, coal began to reach Lincolnshire more cheaply than by road from Newark.

Other industries also stimulated the country's improving waterways with the growing number of brewers in Burton using the Trent to carry their products to the Humber, and Josiah Wedgwood in the Potteries and Matthew Boulton in Birmingham supporting the construction of a canal between the Trent at Sawley and the Mersey which opened in 1777. Nottingham was then placed in an enviable position when the Trent was connected to the River Severn via the Stafford & Worcester Canal and the River Thames via the Grand Junction Canal, the latter giving direct access to London. This connection did reduce the importance of the Trent downstream of Nottingham somewhat, but large quantities of coal continued to reach Gainsborough and Hull for coastal shipment to the capital.

Roads

Roads were also vital to the town's development and, although the impression is always given that they were usually impassable and unsafe, many of the county's routes on sandstone were kept in good repair. Improvements by Turnpike Trusts, carried out in the early 1700s and then again in the late 18th century, enhanced Nottingham's importance despite the building of a number of new bridges across the Trent elsewhere. Although rivers and canals still provided the best form of transport for heavy materials, other goods such as hosiery, lace, people and mail, travelled by road. One of the most prominent road improvements in Nottingham was the elevation, on multiple arches, of the Flood Road (London Road) leading south from the town, (the route traditionally used for transporting coal from the Strelley area to the Trent). By the beginning of the 19th century, businessmen could take advantage of fast and regular stage-coach services to London, Leicester, Coventry, Cambridge, Leeds and Derby, and, just before the Midland Counties Railway opened its line to Nottingham, over 30 stage-coaches were making timetabled journeys daily as far afield as Newcastle and Edinburgh, Manchester and Liverpool amongst others.

Hosiery and Lace Production

By the early 18th century the manufacture of hosiery on framework-knitting machines was one of the town's most important trades and, when James Hargreaves was forced out of Lan-

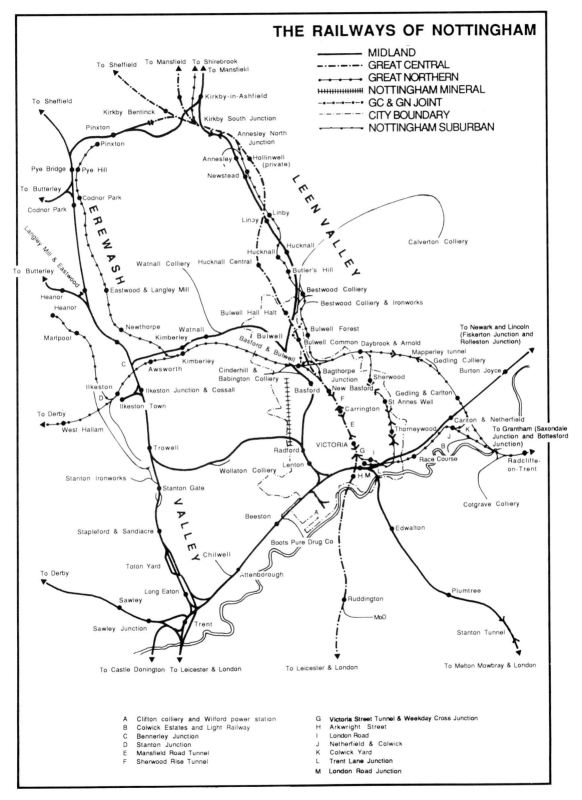

THE RAILWAYS OF NOTTINGHAM

————————	MIDLAND
—·—··—·—·	GREAT CENTRAL
—•—•—•—•	GREAT NORTHERN
++++++++++++	NOTTINGHAM MINERAL
—•—•—•—•	GC & GN JOINT
—·—·—·—·	CITY BOUNDARY
—•—•—•—•	NOTTINGHAM SUBURBAN

To Sheffield
To Mansfield
To Shirebrook
To Mansfield
Kirkby-in-Ashfield
To Sheffield
Kirkby Bentinck
Kirkby South Junction
Pinxton
Annesley North Junction
Pinxton
Annesley
Hollinwell (private)
Pye Bridge
Pye Hill
Newstead
To Butterley
Codnor Park
Linby
Linby
Hucknall
To Butterley
Codnor Park
Hucknall
Hucknall Central
Langley Mill & Eastwood
Watnall Colliery
Hucknall Central
Butler's Hill
To Butterley
Eastwood & Langley Mill
Bestwood Colliery
Heanor
Bestwood Colliery & Ironworks
Heanor
Bulwell Hall Halt
Marlpool
Newthorpe
Watnall
Bulwell Forest
To Newark and Lincoln (Fiskerton Junction and Rolleston Junction)
Kimberley
Bulwell
Mapperley tunnel
Gedling Colliery
Basford & Bulwell
Bulwell Common
Daybrook & Arnold
C
Awsworth
Cinderhill & Babington Colliery
Bagthorpe Junction
Sherwood
Burton Joyce
Kimberley
Basford
New Basford
Gedling & Carlton
Ilkeston
Ilkeston Junction & Cossall
St Annes Well
Carlton & Netherfield
D
Carrington
Thorneywood
To Grantham (Saxondale Junction and Bottesford Junction)
To Derby
Ilkeston Town
E
J
K
West Hallam
B
Trowell
Radford
VICTORIA
Race Course
Radcliffe-on-Trent
Lenton
G
Stanton Ironworks
Wollaton Colliery
H M
Stanton Gate
Cotgrave Colliery
Beeston
A
Stapleford & Sandiacre
Edwalton
Boots Pure Drug Co
To Derby
Chilwell
Toton Yard
Attenborough
Plumtree
Long Eaton
Sawley
Ruddington
Sawley Junction
Trent
MoD
Stanton Tunnel
To Castle Donington
To Leicester & London
To Leicester & London
To Melton Mowbray & London

VALLEY

EREWASH

LEEN VALLEY

A	Clifton colliery and Wilford power station	G	Victoria Street Tunnel & Weekday Cross Junction
B	Colwick Estates and Light Railway	H	Arkwright Street
C	Bennerley Junction	I	London Road
D	Stanton Junction	J	Netherfield & Colwick
E	Mansfield Road Tunnel	K	Colwick Yard
F	Sherwood Rise Tunnel	L	Trent Lane Junction
		M	London Road Junction

cashire in 1767, it was to Nottingham that he turned to experiment further with his 'spinning jenny' machine. Richard Arkwright was also attracted to the town at exactly the same time in order to set up his horse-powered 'water-frame' to spin warp yarn. The inventions of both these men helped shape the Industrial Revolution, although the effects of Arkwright's factory system did not take hold in Nottingham until the mid-1800s. Arkwright turned to Derbyshire to establish his factories but others, such as George Robinson, built a series of cotton mills along the River Leen.

The production of lace by machine, for which Nottingham is still well known, began in the late 18th century. At first plain net was made in small quantities on modified framework-knitting machines, the patterns embroidered on by hand. Then, in the first decade of the 19th century, the inventions of John Heathcoat and John Levers revolutionised manufacture, and the widespread use of their machines led to a boom in the domestic lace industry in the 1820s.

This, and the success of the hosiery industry, encouraged large scale migration into Nottingham, the population increasing approximately five fold in the hundred years after 1730. But,

due to the survival of common land around the town, Nottingham still occupied its mediæval boundaries, and overcrowding led to squalid living and working conditions. Until more land could be released for building, the villages around the town, such as Radford and Lenton, grew more quickly than Nottingham. Attacks by Luddites were one manifestation of the frustration of a select group of employees with poor social conditions and low pay but, in 1831, general resentment focused by the passage of the Electoral Reform bill through Parliament led to the burning of Nottingham Castle. A year later, as if to underline the misery, 300 people died of cholera. It was during this period that some of the first serious attempts were being made to promote standard gauge railways into Nottingham.

Below:
Ex-GN 4-4-0 No 4075 pulls away from Nottingham Victoria under the signal gantry at the north end of the station in the mid-1920s with a train of empty coaching stock. At the end of World War 2 this locomotive as No 2000 was shedded at Grantham and selected for working officers' saloons.
T. G. Hepburn/Rail Archive Stephenson

1. 1600-1836 Early Lines

One of the first documented uses of railways in this country occurs in Nottinghamshire when wooden rails were laid from Huntingdon Beaumont's pits in Wollaton to Nottingham by 1604. This pioneering railway does not appear to have spawned any imitators, and it was not until 1764 that the next reference occurs, this time to a waggon way between Nuthall Colliery and Nottingham. But it was competition in the sale of coal from Nottinghamshire, Derbyshire and Leicestershire which provided the real stimulus to railway development, and looking just at early railways within the county would be historically misleading.

The mining of coal around the Erewash Valley ignored county boundaries, and there were significant developments on the Derbyshire side of the River Erewash at Butterley which are vital to the story. Here, William Jessop and Benjamin Outram were partners in the Butterley Co ironworks, (originally Benjamin Outram & Co from 1790 to 1807). Jessop was responsible for the construction, in 1793-94, of the 'Forest Line' of the Leicester Navigation which connected the Leicestershire collieries around Swannington and Coleorton with a canal between Thringstone and Nanpantan, and then on from there by rail to Loughborough. Coal from the Erewash Valley collieries sold well in Leicestershire, and Jessop's canal and railway were built specifically to promote local coal. The railway was laid with T-section rails, but his partner Benjamin Outram championed L-section plateways, and Jessop found himself using this type of rail for the Little Eaton Gangway in Derbyshire built between 1793 and 1795.

Plateways became more familiar than railways at this period acting as feeder lines from collieries to the Cromford, Erewash and Nottingham canals but, despite this, a significant boost to railway building occurred in 1817. The aim this time was to send coal northwards into Mansfield, and stone and limestone from that town to markets further south via the rivers Trent and Soar. To facilitate this, a railway was promoted in 1813 between Mansfield and Pinxton Wharf on a branch of the Cromford Canal, and this was the first Nottinghamshire railway bill to be successfully steered through Parliament, receiving the Royal Assent on 16 June 1817. The line was engineered by William Jessop's son Josias, and was laid with cast-iron fishbellied rail on stone blocks. The line opened with much public celebration on 13 April 1819 when a pile of Pinxton coal was ceremonially burnt in Mansfield market place.

The Mansfield & Pinxton Railway may not seem at first relevant to the story of Nottingham's railways. But it was the promotion of railways southwards from Pinxton, through the important coal producing district of the Erewash Valley to Leicester, which directly influenced the position of Nottingham on the emerging national railway network. The situation would have been considerably different had the Leen Valley been producing coal at this time and railways had been promoted from Mansfield southwards along this route to Nottingham and Leicester.

The first main line railways

The construction, during 1822-25, and the opening of the Stockton & Darlington Railway, in September 1825, stimulated a general wave of 'railway enthusiasm' over the whole country. In 1824-25 a 'Grand Junction Railway' was proposed to serve Birmingham, Derby, Sheffield, Leeds and Wakefield, with branches to Manchester, Goole and Nottingham. Despite involving the eminent engineers James Walker and Josias Jessop, and inviting applications for shares in Birmingham, Manchester, Sheffield and Nottingham, the project came to nothing.

At the same time a 'London Northern Railroad' was promoted and two alternative routes considered for the line. One struck northeast from London by way of Cambridge, Peterborough and Oakham to Loughborough where branch lines would continue to Derby and Nottingham and beyond to Cromford and Manchester. The other would pass through Northampton with a branch to Coventry, Birmingham, Leicester and Derby, from where another branch would extend to Nottingham. In May 1825 the plans were reduced to a line between London and Cromford (there to link with the Cromford & High Peak Railway), but although engineers'

reports and plans were completed, the project was shelved. Both the GJR and the LNR were too ambitious for the railway technology then available, and tried to appeal to too many disparate investors.

Locally the stimulii to improved transport links was not national considerations but still the battle between Notts-Derby and Leicestershire coal. The opening of the Stockton & Darlington Railway in 1825 had a direct influence on the promotion of a modest, but very practical railway between the Leicestershire coalfields around Swannington and the county town of Leicester. A visit to the Darlington railway in 1828 persuaded the promoters of the Leicester & Swannington Railway that their line was feasible. The young Robert Stephenson was appointed engineer, and the line was authorised by Parliament in May 1830.

This obviously dismayed the colliery owners in the Erewash Valley, who, for the moment, had to content themselves with a revival of the London Northern Railroad plans at the end of 1830. Fortunately for them, after reconsideration of the practicalities of such an ambitious undertaking, the Board of Management concentrated on what they felt was likely to be the most remunerative part of their scheme — the line between Cromford and Leicester. This section of line had already been surveyed by Josias Jessop during the initial surveys of the London Northern Railroad in 1824-25 and, naturally, the proposed railway was to pass along the Erewash Valley. Disappointingly, although the plans were submitted to Parliament at the end of 1830, they proceeded no further.

Nearly two years later on 17 July 1832 the first section of the Leicester & Swannington Railway opened and, realising the war had started,

the Erewash Valley coal owners at one of their regular meetings in the Sun Inn, Eastwood, on 16 August, plotted railway retaliation. On the 27th of the same month a special meeting was called at the George Inn, Alfreton, and it was here that plans were made public for an ambitious extension of the Mansfield & Pinxton Railway to Leicester. A Provisional Committee was set up, and at another meeting in Alfreton on 15 October utilising the plans of the London Northern Railroad, the 'Midland Counties Railway' was launched.

But railway development had already run on apace since the plans of the LNR had been drawn up. The steam locomotive had proved itself beyond doubt on the Liverpool & Manchester Railway (which had opened in September 1830). That railway had also shown the tremendous potential of passenger traffic and, as a result, proposals for colliery lines were giving way to plans for 'inter-city' railways. Even the Mansfield & Pinxton Railway had started to carry passengers by 1832. Responding to this trend, the MCR suggested branches leaving its main line at Long Eaton along the valley of the Derwent to Derby, and along the Trent valley to Nottingham. Thoughts also turned to extending from Leicester to join the projected London & Birmingham Railway at either Rugby or Northampton. As all these ideas were simply grafted on to Jessop's original survey of 1824-25, it could be argued with some justification that Nottingham's railway connection was no more than an afterthought. This afterthought is further substantiated by the fact that the October 1832 MCR prospectus only mentions Nottingham and Derby briefly at the end. And then it has to admit that the new railway between Derby and Leicester would be two miles longer

than the existing Turnpike road, and one mile longer than by road between Nottingham and Leicester.

Nevertheless, it did fall to Nottingham solicitors Messrs Leeson & Gell to issue the first formal notice of the MCR's intention to deposit plans for the Parliamentary Session of 1833. Unfortunately, these plans did not formally become a bill, and George Rennie was asked to reassess them with William Jessop (brother of Josias). Some slight modifications were made and plans were deposited again in November 1833. These plans included the extension from Leicester to Rugby and proposed alternative terminal stations in Nottingham on London Road and Castle Gate.

Influential local support came from William Felkin and William Hannay, who set up a committee to encourage current railway plans. Hannay was a hosiery manufacturer and became a director of the MCR. Felkin, born in Ilkeston in 1795, began his career as a London agent selling hosiery and, by the 1840s, had established his own lacemaking factory in Nottingham and Beeston. He became a very important local personality, was mayor of Nottingham in 1851 and 1852, and wrote the *History of the Machine Wrought Hosiery & Lace Manufacture* in 1867. However, insufficient funds were forthcoming for the 1834 Session and this delayed any presentation of the MCR proposals before Parliament for another year. Undaunted, modified plans were submitted for the next Session at Westminster, but once again they foundered.

Following this series of failed attempts, the Lancashire investors in the railway decided to take matters in their own hands. In August 1835, at their suggestion, the railway's chairman, Matthew Babington, approached Charles Vignoles, who had worked as engineer for the Liverpool & Manchester Railway, and Vignoles was duly appointed engineer of the MCR. By the

Top:
Tinted lithograph, c1850, of the MCR's cast-iron bridge across the River Trent and the portal of Redhill Tunnel. In the right foreground is the River Soar. *Ironbridge Gorge Museum Trust/Elton Collection/AE185.802*

Right:
Engraving, c1850, of the Midland Railway's second Nottingham station on Station Street looking southeast. *NCCLSL/2109*

end of the year he had resurveyed the whole line and made considerable alterations. The junction curves at Long Eaton were enlarged and, in Nottingham, alternative stations were proposed in Wheeler Gate as well as on London Road. The plans were deposited with the appropriate authorities in November 1835 but, once again, they were slightly out of step with current railway thinking and, under the watchful eye of the influential Lancashire financiers, vulnerable to their changing ideas.

Vignoles had plans for an extension of the MCR from Pinxton northwards to Clay Cross and Chesterfield and, in February 1836, a plan was issued showing a further extension to Sheffield, Wakefield and Leeds. But George Stephenson had also been surveying an independent line between Derby and Leeds during 1835 — the North Midland Railway. Conflict was inevitable. Derby obviously championed Stephenson's line and, with it, the promise of a direct railway into Yorkshire. The town was also aware that, with the MCR and the projected Birmingham & Derby Junction Railway, it had the potential to become an important railway centre. Combined with opposition from the canal interests in the Erewash Valley, the Lancashire investors feared that the MCR project might founder yet again, so, as Frederick Williams in his colourful Victorian prose records in *Midland Railway; Its Rise and Progress*, '...the substantial assistance of moneyed men of the North, whose only anxiety was to secure a great through route to the South, and who cared little for the solicitude of a few coal-owners in a remote Nottinghamshire valley...' forced the abandonment of the entire Erewash Valley section of the MCR. At a stroke the MCR plans were beheaded; Jessop's colliery line had been sacrificed for a more fashionable passenger line, and it was to be another 12 years before a railway was built along the Erewash Valley. An agreement was reached between the NMR and the MCR whereby the former would channel all traffic from Derby to London via the MCR and, with an irony not lost on its original Erewash Valley promoters, the MCR bill finally succeeded in passing through the House of Lords, receiving the Royal Assent on 21 June 1836.

Ex-MR 0-6-0 No 43580 taking empty coal wagons northwards along the ex-MR Erewash Valley line passed Bennerley Junction in May 1954. In the background the ex-GN viaduct carrying the Derbyshire & North Staffordshire Extension lines between Awsworth and Ilkeston. *J. F. Oxley*

2. 1837-44 The Midland Counties Railway

It was along the natural corridor formed by the Trent that the first main line railway approached Nottingham. As access to Derby was along the neighbouring Derwent valley, construction of the MCR between these two towns was an easy affair, and this is where work began.

The first contract was let to John Taylor, Thomas Johnson and Henry Sharp of Long Eaton on 22 May 1837 for the section of line between Nottingham and Long Eaton (£35,236). Manufacture of cast-iron for the Trent bridge was entrusted to the local Butterley Co, but, interestingly, the erection of this structure, along with the construction of the formation between Derby and Loughborough and the junction at Long Eaton (Trent), was awarded to a Lancashire firm, William Mackenzie of Leyland (£166,678). This was the firm which, in 1829, had excavated the difficult tunnel between Edge Hill and Crown Street in Liverpool for the Liverpool & Manchester Railway.

Between July and September 1837, 423 men were employed on construction work between Derby and Nottingham. The figure reached a

Below:
The MR opened its railway along the Leen Valley in October 1848, and this is the goods yard at Basford station on that line, with 0-6-0 No 2427 posed for the camera of the official railway company photographer on 3 April 1922. *Crown Copyright courtesy National Railway Museum/DY12483*

poak of 922, with 76 horses, by the end of the year. By the following spring work was sufficiently advanced for contracts to be considered for the supply of wrought-iron rails and cast-iron chairs, or 'pedestals' as they were described in the advertisement of 3 February. Contracts for laying the permanent way were awarded to the firms who had undertaken the earthworks, and the first stone blocks were laid at Chilwell in August. The permanent way between Nottingham and Derby was estimated to have cost £82,000. On 5 June the contract to build Nottingham station was awarded to Drewry, Hall & Dale for £5,673 3s 1d and the Directors, at their Annual General Meeting that month, confidently anticipated an opening on 1 May 1839. Work was progressing with the Trent bridge and Redhill tunnel and, at the end of October, advertisements appeared for two 'Principal Clerks' for Derby and Nottingham stations at a salary of £150 per annum each.

The promised opening at the beginning of May did not happen but, that month, a number of Directors and their friends were treated to high speed trial runs between Nottingham and Long Eaton. The first was in a specially prepared carriage, and the journey of seven miles was reported to have been achieved in just 16min.

The ceremonial opening took place on Thursday 29 May when according to *The Railway Times*: '...Nottingham poured forth its thousands upon thousands of anxious spectators — some almost covering the meadows near the line of road — others occupying the various eminences in the park, whilst hundreds more flocked to the windows and the tops of almost every building which commanded a view of the novel and imposing spectacle.'

At 12.30pm the first train of four first-class and two second-class carriages behind locomo-tive *Sunbeam* steamed out of Nottingham station for Derby followed at intervals of about 10min by three others. The whole route was lined with people who witnessed the special trains speeding by at well over 30mph. In the late afternoon Nottingham played host to the returning Directors and other guests, who were treated to a celebratory 'cold collation'.

Nottingham station

In Vignoles' MCR surveys of 1835, it had been suggested that the line could be turned sharply northwards across the Nottingham Canal, near Wilford bridge, to a station on Wheeler Gate very close to the Market Place but, apparently, this option was lost during the Parliamentary debates. In February the MCR had laid its plans before the Town Council for a station site on common land in the Meadows, south of the Nottingham Canal, and, with little opposition, the Council had agreed to sell land there in March. There was no existing road to the site; in fact no real access at all. The only Turnpike road running south from the town, London Road (or the Flood Road), was over a quarter of a mile away to the east.

This awkward station site immediately committed the Council to the construction of a new road from London Road to the station (Station Street), an extension of Carrington Street southwards and an expensive bridge over the Nottingham Canal. Needless to say, the new roads and bridge were not ready for the opening of the railway, and passengers had to reach the station over a canal bridge to the west and then through the railway yard.

The station was a very modest affair compared with Derby's. The latter had a façade 1,050ft long and a single platform for the use of

Left:
The Ambergate, Nottingham & Boston & Eastern Junction Railway's new terminus on London Road nearing completion in 1856, recorded by one of the town's first photographers Samuel Bourne.
NCCLSL/26066

Above:
The wrought-iron roof trusses forming the original train shed of the AN&B&EJR's London Road terminus, photographed on 17 October 1992. *Author*

the three companies approaching from the north, south and east. The offices at Nottingham station, built of Darley Dale stone, looked like a superior domestic house. Its restrained classical façade was a mere 90ft wide, with a single front

door. The right-hand wing of the building was occupied by the first and second-class booking office, whilst the left-hand wing contained the Boardroom and clerk's offices. At the back of the building was a ladies' waiting room, and behind this was a simple trainshed of two pitched iron roofs, the town side and central valley supported on nine cast-iron columns each, and the southside on a brick wall pierced by eight small windows.

The First 'Railway Mania'

Both Nottingham and Derby were to have been served by terminal stations but, with the passing of the Acts for the North Midland and Birmingham & Derby Junction railways at the same time as that for the MCR, Derby immediately became a railway hub and not the end of a branch line spoke like Nottingham. The consequences of Derby's sudden railway gain at Nottingham's expense were immediately apparent, but not always understood. One councillor attributed the town's failure to secure a direct north-south line to its 'neglect and indifference'.

Given the geographical position of the town, this was certainly not the case and, although with hindsight we know that Nottingham remained the end of the line until 1846, it was not due totally to indifference. In May 1836 Nottingham Town Council had established a special committee to monitor railway projects. Vignoles had not given up on his Erewash Valley line, introducing modified plans for the 1837 Parliamentary Session and, by the end of that year, there were also two firm proposals to link Nottingham directly with Hull and Sheffield. The Hull railway was promoted in March, running via Lincoln and Newark, and the MCR itself anticipated a successful link with this indepen-

Left:
The AN&B&EJR's cast-iron bridge across the River Trent was finished in the early months of 1850. WD 2-10-0 No 90000, seen here on 6 July 1955 heading east with a coal train from Colwick yard, is crossing the brick viaduct which replaced the wooden structure. *J. F. Oxley*

Left:
The main block of the substantial station building at Trent, opened by the MR in May 1862, and photographed shortly before closure in 1968.
T. G. Hepburn/Rail Archive Stephenson

dent company at Nottingham. In November plans were deposited for a line northwards along the Leen Valley towards Sheffield — the Midland Grand Junction Railway. Despite its 'grand' title, this was obviously not as well supported and, nearly a year later on 16 October 1838 at a public meeting in the White Lion Hotel, Nottingham, the town's mayor John Heard acting as chairman had to confess '...that he was not at all acquainted with the projected plans...' and would have to let the public decide for themselves whether the railway was worthy of support or not. As it transpired 1838 was a barren year for Nottingham in Parliament; Vignoles' Erewash Valley line failed again, and neither the HL&NR nor MGJR plans were successful.

The early years to 1844

Despite fares of 4s first-class and 2s 6d second-class between Nottingham and Derby, higher than those charged by coach operators, and no third-class carriages available until September 1839, many more people than expected travelled on the MCR in the opening months. At first an average of 300 people per day crowded into the trains. When fares were reduced by 6d at the end of June the daily figure increased to 900 and, at the Annual General Meeting of the company held in August, it was reported that, between 4 June and 2 August, the railway had carried 26,546 passengers, generating a revenue of £3,022 18s 10d. Obviously there was the novelty of the new line to be considered, but receipts remained healthy throughout the year with an average of 2,500 people being carried every week. The local papers as well as *The Railway Times* avidly reported the progress and,

when third-class carriages, little more than open wagons with no seats, for the 'poorer classes', were introduced, the *Derby Reporter* commented '...that cannot be much inconvenience in so short a distance [and] they only go by the first train in the morning and the last in the evening'.

On 5 May 1840 the MCR was opened between Trent Junction and Leicester. Four trains each way on weekdays and two on Sundays were operated over the whole line from this date. This led to the immediate withdrawal of the three daily road coaches between Leicester and Nottingham, the last journey of *The Lark* from Leicester being not only a sad, but a tragic affair. The coach was driven for the last time by its regular driver Mr Frisby of Nottingham, and he was accompanied by Mr Pearson (recently made redundant as driver of *The Times* coach which had been withdrawn between Nottingham and London). Both men were what the Victorians called 'steady' men, Pearson having worked regularly between Nottingham and Northampton without incident and never missed a day's work in eight years. But the occasion encouraged Frisby to allow more than the regulation number of outside passengers, and to drive his team too quickly. At Coates Mill, just beyond Loughborough, the coach overturned at speed on a bend in the road killing one of the passengers and injuring many of the others. Frisby was badly hurt and Pearson died later at Loughborough. It was a tragic epitaph to the golden age of stage-coach travel.

The extension of the MCR to join the London & Birmingham Railway at Rugby was finally opened on 1 July 1840 and, as is well known, this triggered a financially damaging fares war with the Birmingham & Derby Junction Railway. Nottingham seems to have been little affected by this, although it appears that during the summer of 1840 goods traffic between Nottingham and London was being sent via Derby and the B&DJR until agreement could be reached with the L&B for the transfer of traffic at Rugby. From 17 August a night mail train was run in each direction between London, Leicester, Loughborough, Nottingham, Derby, Sheffield, Leeds and York; the Nottingham departure for the capital being at 10.39pm and the return arrival at 3.9am.

The station at Nottingham was still difficult to reach from the town, the MCR having pressed the Town Council in October 1839 to extend Carrington Street by building a bridge over the Nottingham Canal. At first the Council's Carrington Street Bridge Committee was reluctant to accede to the railway company's demand for a bridge 50ft wide. However, when the MCR offered to contribute £3,000 towards the costs if the Council withdrew its opposition to the level crossing at Wilford Road (they had wanted a road bridge), a compromise was achieved. The shallow cast-iron spans were manufactured by Cort & Co at their Rutland Foundry in Granby Street, Nottingham, to designs by H. M. Wood. The foundation stone was laid in October 1841 and the Carrington Street canal bridge finally opened the following year, having cost £5,945.

This was the first of a number of road improvements carried out by the Town Council in the 19th century. For the visit of Queen Victoria and the Prince Consort on 4 December 1843 a new road was built parallel to Station Street, south of the railway. This new road curved eastwards away from the station to join the Flood Road (London Road), and was appropriately christened Queen's Road in honour of the event. Access between the Market Place and the station was improved when Albert Street was completed at a cost of £8,000 in 1846, but further improvements were difficult to achieve and generally roads remained narrow and a constant cause of complaint.

As well as influencing the growth of the town's road network, no matter how hesitantly, the railway also indirectly helped stimulate Nottingham's building trade. The siting of the station on common land to the south of the town provided a significant impetus towards the enclosing of all such land. This was finally given Parliamentary approval in 1845. 1,069 acres were dealt with, and hundreds of plots of land were freed for the building of much needed domestic housing and factories. The Act also gave the Council powers to regulate sanitation and lay out streets no less than 30ft wide.

In the following two decades, as the Meadows area south of the station was extensively built upon, another new road, Arkwright Street, was gradually extended southwards from Queen's Road to provide a through route into the town from the Town Council's fine new cast-iron bridge over the River Trent (opened on 25 July 1871). Arkwright Street and Queen's Road (later becoming part of Carrington Street) then superseded London Road as the main thoroughfare into Nottingham from the south, and remained so until the drastic reorganisation of the city's road system in the 1960s and 1970s.

This poor quality image is included because photographs of the AN&B&EJR's original timber viaduct across the Trent Valley at Radcliffe-on-Trent, which was replaced in 1912, are rare. The river is obviously in flood as a LNWR train heads for Nottingham. *NCCLSL*

3. 1845 The Railway Mania

1845 is famous, or infamous, as the year when thousands of people speculated in hundreds of new railway companies. The railways projected in the first half of the year had comparatively sensible aims but, as the number of proposed railways grew after the Parliamentary Session had started, it became obvious that most of their aspirations were completely impossible to achieve. *The Railway Chronicle* with uncharacteristic humour summed up the period when in October it placed an advertisement of its own inviting shares in 'The Land's End & John O'Groat's Atmospheric Railway', accompanied by a very convincing prospectus as to the merits of the new 'direct' line.

For those Midlands schemes which actually reached the stage of depositing plans for the 1845 or 1846 Parliamentary Session, other than raising capital, the most difficult obstacle to realising their aims was the opposition of the recently created Midland Railway. The MR was an amalgamation of the MCR, NMR and the B&DJR, all carefully managed by George Hudson. As Chairman of the new company, he and his supporters with far more resources than any new speculative venture, successfully bought off, or defeated at the Parliamentary committee stages, most of their rivals. The battle against the London & York Railway, which eventually became the Great Northern Railway, was particularly fierce and acrimonious, and was directly responsible for the very rapid construction of

the MR's line between Nottingham and Lincoln, a railway Hudson and the Board were determined would reach both Newark and Lincoln before the GN. The MR's Syston & Peterborough line was also promoted with the aim of reaching Peterborough ahead of the GN.

The overlapping routes of many independent local railway projects confirm the excesses of the Railway Mania, and this combined with the fact that Hudson defeated almost all newcomers, unfortunately obscures the merits of those unsuccessful proposals which might have been economically viable and were backed by men who were not just speculators. Looking at the list of those schemes which affected Nottingham, a number were surveyed and had obtained the services of notable and respected engineers. Nottingham Council certainly took most of the projects seriously, setting up a special Railway Committee to investigate the plans, and reiterating the Council's desire for a direct line to London, Sheffield and Leeds.

Ambergate, Nottingham & Boston & Eastern Junction Railway

Engineer: John Urpeth Rastrick
Formed by the amalgamation of the Nottingham, Erewash Valley, Ambergate & Manchester Railway, the Nottingham, Vale of Belvoir &

Left:
Trent Station South Junction looking northeast as seen by the official MR photographer on 8 August 1896. The signalbox was unusual in having a brick base as the majority of MR boxes were completely wooden. The trees on the right of the scene mark the route of the independent goods lines from Toton completed a few years later.
Crown Copyright, courtesy National Railway Museum/DY390

Grantham Railway, and the Nottingham & Boston Railway on 18 September 1845, with an agreement to purchase the Nottingham and Nottingham-Grantham canals: see below. Royal Assent gained on 16 July 1846. (See Chapter 4).

Birmingham, Nottingham, Gainsborough & Hull Railway

A proposed link from the MR at Whitacre (east of Birmingham) through Ashby-de-la-Zouch to join the MR again at Long Eaton, and then using either the proposed Nottingham & Gainsborough Railway (see below) or along the MR's Parliamentary-approved Nottingham & Lincoln line to reach Gainsborough.

Provisional Committee of 63.

Grand Union Railway

Engineer: Charles Vignoles
A line from the MR at Nottingham, across the River Trent near West Bridgford, to Holme Pierrepont, through Radcliffe-on-Trent, Bingham, Bottesford, Grantham and on to Spalding, Sutton Bridge and King's Lynn, there to join the proposed Lynn & East Dereham Railway.

An extension to Boston was advertised in June 1845, the railway being named the Nottingham, Boston & Grand Union Junction Railway.

Provisional Committee of 43, increased to 79 by the end of 1845, including the Mayor of Nottingham.

Great Leeds & London Direct Railway

A project rather than a railway, with the aim of connecting various existing, proposed and/or sanctioned lines including the MR's Nottingham & Lincoln and Syston & Peterborough lines, to form a continuous route between Leeds and London.

Enormous Provisional Committee of 237, most of whom had interests in other Railway Mania companies.

London & Nottingham Railway

Engineers: G. H. Gregory, Thomas Hawksley and Nathaniel Briant
Intended to start from Bedford on whichever railway Parliament sanctioned there from London, via Kettering and Melton Mowbray, to Nottingham. At Nottingham it would connect with one of the railways proposed north of the town.

Provisional Committee of 70, headed by The Right Hon Digby, Lord Middleton of Wollaton Hall, Nottingham, as well as the Mayor of Nottingham, William Felkin and William Hannay.

Midland Railway

Lines were planned along the Erewash and Leen valleys to the Mansfield & Pinxton Railway, and between Nottingham and Lincoln.

The line between Sawley and Codnor Park had been promoted as the independent Erewash Valley Railway, (receiving the Royal Assent on 4 August 1845), but was constructed and operated by the MR who added further branches after gaining its own Act in 1846.

The Nottingham-Lincoln line was authorised by Act of Parliament on 30 June 1845 followed by the Leen Valley line Act on 16 July 1846.

Nottingham, Birmingham & Coventry Railway

Acting engineer: Elijah Galloway
Proposal for a line from the MR at Long Eaton station, via Castle Donington, Ashby-de-la-Zouch, and Measham to Market Bosworth, here to join the proposed Tamworth & Leicester Railway's Birmingham branch, and then on to Nuneaton to join the proposed Coventry, Nuneaton, Birmingham & Leicester Railway.

Provisional Committee of 35, increased to 67 later in 1845, including the Mayor of Nottingham and William Hannay.

Nottingham & Boston Railway

Engineer: Sir John Rennie
As well as emphasising the proposed line's potential for carrying the agricultural products of Lincolnshire into Nottingham, speedily and in more quantity than by way of the River Witham, along the River Trent, or along the Nottingham-Grantham canal, the prospectus also stated:

'A very considerable amount of the vast stable produce of Nottingham, Derby, Loughborough, Leicester and the neigh-bourhood which is exported to Belgium, Holland, Denmark, Germany and other parts of the Baltic, is now conveyed by the circuitous and expensive route to Hull and London, and thence, after repeated removals by ship or steamer, to its destination; whereas, on the completion of this line, it would be transmitted direct to Boston, and thence to the before-mentioned places, in much less time, and at a much less expense.'

It also recorded that 62,000 tons of goods ranging from corn and malt to timber, including 35,000 tons of coal, were transported annually between Nottingham and Grantham, by river and canal.

Provisional Committee of 31, including the Mayor of Boston and William Hannay of Nottingham.

Formally amalgamated with the Nottingham, Erewash Valley, Ambergate & Manchester Railway and the Nottingham, Vale of Belvoir & Grantham Railway on 18 September 1845 to form the **Ambergate, Nottingham & Boston & Eastern Junction Railway**, with an agreement to purchase the Nottingham and Nottingham-Grantham canals.

Below:
GN 0-4-2 No 953 pauses at Basford & Bulwell station on the Derbyshire & North Staffordshire Extension lines with the 1.32pm Grantham to Derby train on 20 November 1913. *F. H. Gillford/John Marshall Collection*

Left:
Newthorpe & Greasley station on the GN's Erewash Valley line, photographed in July 1951 looking southeast. *Douglas Thompson/Robert Humm & Co*

Nottingham, Erewash Valley, Ambergate & Manchester Railway

Engineer: John Urpeth Rastrick

A line from Nottingham to the proposed Manchester, Buxton, Matlock & Midlands Junction Railway at Ambergate.

Provisional Committee of 44, including two directors of the Erewash Canal Co, and 13 directors of the Cromford and Nottingham Canal companies.

Formally amalgamated with the Nottingham & Boston Railway and the Nottingham, Vale of Belvoir & Grantham Railway on 18 September 1845 to form the **Ambergate, Nottingham & Boston & Eastern Junction Railway**, with an agreement to purchase the Nottingham and Nottingham-Grantham canals.

Nottingham & Gainsborough Railway

This company's proposed line was to start 'near' Nottingham, and run via Lenton and the Leen Valley to Bulwell, Oxton, Tuxford and Gainsborough.

Provisional Committee of 58, including the Mayor of Nottingham.

After a meeting of shareholders on 21 November 1845 it was decided to abandon the project.

Nottingham & Mansfield Railway

Engineer: Joseph Gibbs
Surveyor: George Sanderson

Formed on 8 April 1845 after a meeting in Nottingham, this company intended to build a line from the MR near Nottingham through Lenton, Basford, Bulwell, Hucknall Torkard, Selston, Kirkby-in-Ashfield to terminate in Sutton-in-Ashfield. To incorporate the existing Mansfield & Pinxton Railway, as well as forming a junction with the proposed Newark & Sheffield Railway at Teversal.

Provisional Committee of 52, including the Mayor of Nottingham and William Felkin of Nottingham.

At the beginning of September an extension to join the MR at Clay Cross was advertised and a new company registered as the **Nottingham, Mansfield & Midlands Junction Railway**. At the same time the advertisement for the new railway in the *Railway Chronicle* announced the railway's amalgamation with the Nottingham, Erewash Valley, Ambergate & Manchester Railway and the Nottingham, Vale of Belvoir & Grantham Railway, although this does not appear to have been formalised. A few days later the Boston, Newark & Sheffield Railway also announced an 'amalgamation of interests' with the new company. By the end of 1845 both this company and the Nottingham, Mansfield & Midlands Junction Railway had been leased to the Sheffield, Ashton-under-Lyne & Manchester Railway. The Nottingham & Mansfield Railway was bought off by the MR in July 1846, for £40,000 of its stock.

Nottingham Mineral Railway

Engineer: Woodhouse

A proposal to extend an existing line connecting North, Wakefield & Co's coalpits at Babbington near Kimberley, and Cinderhill (sunk 1841-43 and eventually named Babbington colliery) through Whitemoor to a wharf on the Nottingham Canal near Radford, the earliest section having been constructed in the late 1830s and worked by a steam locomotive. The new lines would have reached Basford, Carrington and a site on Mansfield Road close to where Victoria station was built. Early in 1846 the promoters of the new line asked the Ambergate, Nottingham & Boston & Eastern Junction Railway to build the line, but the railway company only agreed to construct a branch from its joint line with the MR at Basford to the pit at Cinderhill. This branch was eventually built by the colliery company in 1852 and purchased by the MR in 1877.

Nottingham & South Staffordshire Railway

A short line intended to join Long Eaton (presumably the MR there) to Alrewas on the proposed South Staffordshire Junction Railway.

Nottingham, Vale of Belvoir & Grantham Railway

A line from the Nottingham, Erewash Valley, Ambergate & Manchester Railway to Grantham.

Formally amalgamated with that company and the Nottingham and Boston Railway on 18 September 1845 to form the **Ambergate, Nottingham & Boston & Eastern Junction Railway**, with an agreement to purchase the Nottingham and Nottingham-Grantham canals.

Below:
A marshalling yard and locomotive sheds for both the GN and the LNWR were opened at Colwick during 1878/1880. This photograph looking southwest shows GN 'L1' 0-8-2T No 139, only a few years old, with the breakdown train in c1908.
F. Moore/Bucknall Collection/Ian Allan Ltd

Peterborough & Nottingham Junction Railway

Consulting engineers: Sir John Rennie and George Rennie
Acting engineer: William Lewin

A line projected to run from Stamford station, on the MR's Syston & Peterborough Railway, to Oakham, Melton Mowbray, Long Clawson and West Bridgford to join the MR at Nottingham.

Provisional Committee of 87, increased to 96 later in 1845 including a considerable number of directors of other Railway Mania companies.

Sheffield, Nottingham & London Direct Railway

Engineers: Sir John Rennie and George Remington

The aim of this railway was to connect Sheffield with Kettering where it was to join the proposed London & Manchester Direct Railway. The advertisement commented that:

> 'It cannot fail to be a matter of surprise that the large and important manufacturing town of Nottingham should so long have remained unaccommodated with a more direct and independent line of railway to London than the existing circuitous route, and that, too, made up of several sections.'

A formidable Provisional Committee of 97 mostly credited with being directors of many other Railway Mania companies.

4. 1846-69 The Years of Growth

In the years after the Railway Mania Nottingham grew rapidly expanding on to the recently enclosed common land surrounding the town. The railways encouraged a new mobility, bringing people in from surrounding villages helping to create the necessary labour force for industry to expand. Between 1841 and 1871 the population rose from 53,201 to 86,600, and the number of houses and factories rose accordingly. Between 1851 and 1856 alone, 2,101 new houses, 74 new factories and 41 warehouses were erected.

In *Whites Nottingham Directory* of 1844 there are 148 lace manufacturers listed, and, by 1868, 195, not to mention the independent machine holders and merchants, and other manufacturers in outlying villages like Radford and Beeston.

During this period lace making moved out of the home and into new purpose-built factories. By 1865 90% of all lace machinery was steam-powered, coal for the boilers being supplied by the railway. The railway further stimulated the lace trade by opening up direct and fast access to London markets, by taking the finished product to ports like Liverpool for export and by bringing in the buyers to view the latest designs of the Nottingham factories. This specialised and skilled trade brought great prosperity to the town and, in typical Victorian fashion, this prosperity was manifested in the grand architecture of the manufacturers' and merchants' houses in areas like The Park to the west of the Castle where building began in 1854, and the proud new factories of the growing Lace Market around St Mary's church. Thomas Adams' lace warehouse in Stoney Street, erected in 1855, was compared to a grand town hall; its architect, T. C. Hine, going on to design the equally grand premises on London Road for the AN&B&EJR.

MR Passenger Facilities at Nottingham

On 3 February 1846, the Nottingham Town Council ordered that the clocks on the Exchange and Town Hall buildings '...be provided with a third hand to mark Railway Time'. Six months later, on 3 August, the ceremonial opening of the line to Lincoln took place and, for 2 years after that, there was the most awkward connection imaginable between the original MCR station and the Lincoln line. From the east, the railway crossed Queen's Road on the level, skirted the south side of the MCR station, and then joined the line to Derby a few hundred yards to the west. At first trains to and from Lincoln had to reverse into and out of the station, until extra platforms were constructed alongside the terminal's southern wall.

The Town Council had opposed the Queen's Road level crossing during the committee stages of the Lincoln line bill's passage through Parliament but, perversely, they objected in November 1845 to a bridge taking the Flood Road (London Road) over the same line, stating that it would '...destroy the uniformity and present handsome appearance of the approach to the Town by the Flood Road.'

Perhaps this apparent inconsistency helped keep the building of a bridge for Queen's Road low on the list of MR priorities. But, equally, Arkwright Street had not yet been constructed from the south of Queen's Road to Trent Bridge, which meant that London Road was still the only route into Nottingham from the south. Plans for the construction of a proper through station, however, quickly became absolutely necessary. It is difficult to understand why these plans did not form part of the Nottingham-Lincoln line bill, especially as the Erewash Valley line also received its Act in 1845 and would obviously channel more traffic into Nottingham. Perhaps the company only realised just how inadequate the existing station would become when the Act for its Leen Valley line received the Royal Assent in July 1846 and, with it, an agreement with the AN&B&EJR to run its trains over this line into the MR's Nottingham station.

Plans of the new station were formally announced to the Town Council on 4 May 1847; the main façade facing Station Street closely resembling the neat classical building provided at Lincoln. There were two platforms separated by two through tracks and the trainsheds were supported on cast-iron columns. Following the opening of the Erewash Valley line on 6 September 1847, passengers had to endure the original

Left:
**Another view from the
same vantage point, the
photographer having turned
to his left to record
Colwick's huge GN
locomotive shed.**
*F. Moore/Bucknall
Collection/Ian Allan Ltd*

MCR station for eight more months before the new premises were opened to traffic on 26 May 1848 followed, five months later on 2 October, by the opening of the Leen Valley line as far as Kirkby-in-Ashfield.

The first passenger service between Nottingham and Codnor Park over the Erewash Valley line consisted of three trains each way during the week. As there was no direct link from the Erewash line towards Derby, passengers could change trains at Long Eaton station. From 9 October 1849, the new Nottingham station began to deal with traffic from Mansfield following the upgrading of the Mansfield & Pinxton line, trains joining the Leen Valley route at Kirkby. A little later on, an extension between Pinxton and Pye Bridge on the Erewash Valley line was completed and Mansfield could then be reached from Nottingham by two routes. Three weekday trains each way, with two on Sundays, began running over the Erewash line between the two towns, via Pye Bridge, on 1 November 1851, although most trains between Nottingham and Mansfield continued to use the shorter Leen Valley route.

These are of course just the cold facts and figures, but it is possible to glean a few insights into the actual day-to-day running of the railway from the official company minutes and newspapers, and the picture is of an organisation not always fully in control of the situation. For example, in October 1848, an unattended engine pushed a number of carriages 15 miles down the Lincoln line before running out of steam at Fiskerton. Two years later AN&B&EJR trains began to work into the MR station from Grantham and, a couple of months after this, the MR's Way & Works Committee found it necessary to comment, uncharacteristically, on the handling of trains at the station, ordering on 3 September 1850, 'That in future Mr Pettifer

the Station Master at Nottingham, do start the Nottingham and Mansfield Train upon the right Line'. This occurred at a time when the railway company had reduced its fares on all local lines and, according to the *Nottingham Journal*, passenger numbers on the Nottingham-Mansfield line had doubled. Five months later, in February the following year, it was agreed to install a bell to signal the arrival of trains perhaps because of this increase in passengers. In June 1851, during what must have been a typical English summer, it was reported that a new porter's and lamp room was needed as the existing room was '...continually flooded', and August proved equally gloomy when Mr Hardy, proprietor of the second-class refreshment room, handed in his notice because his room was 'unfit for the purpose'. This was unfortunate because the station was extremely busy in September and October, many people taking advantage of special trains to and from London for the Great Exhibition in Hyde Park. Working for the MR in Nottingham at this time must have been an exciting experience.

In 1857 the MR completed its link with the GN at Hitchin and began to run its London trains to and from King's Cross instead of Euston. The company then looked to shorten the distance between London and Leeds and presented a bill in the Parliamentary Session of 1859 for an extension of the Erewash Valley line from Pye Bridge to Clay Cross where it would join the former NMR main line. This short extension opened for goods traffic on 1 November 1861, and to passengers on 1 May the following year. After that date through expresses, formerly travelling via Derby, were diverted to the shorter route. The extension did not, of course, alter Nottingham's isolation from the main line, but it did bring main line services a little closer. This was achieved, not by the meagre service of two stopping trains a day between Nottingham and Clay Cross (all extended to Chesterfield in June that year), but by the construction of a station at Trent Junction.

Trent station

In MCR days, most passengers from Nottingham to Leicester and London had to travel to Derby first, although some southbound trains were combined at Trent Junction from Derby and Nottingham, and others divided in the opposite direction. There is evidence to indicate that some passengers also changed trains at the junction and there appears to have been a small platform on the southbound side of the Nottingham line just before it joined the Derby line at the south junction. However, it was not until the building of the Erewash Valley extension that the MR admitted there was a need for a proper interchange station at Trent.

At this time, apart from the original MCR triangle of tracks, the Erewash Valley line running northwards off the eastern side of the triangle — the Leicester-Nottingham line — had created a flat crossing — Platt's Crossing — where it cut across the northern side of the triangle — the Derby-Nottingham line. A north-east junction had also been created — Long Eaton Junction — but, as already mentioned, trains were unable to run directly off the Erewash line to Derby. With the increasing amount of coal emanating from the Erewash coalfield, Platt's Crossing had become a great inconvenience and, although powers had been obtained in 1848 to construct a junction to facilitate a direct link between Derby and the Erewash line which would have also done away with Platt's Crossing, the junctions at Trent remained unaltered. The engineer's brief in 1861 was, therefore, to eliminate the flat crossing and create a set of junctions that would allow trains to approach and leave Trent station from all directions.

Plans for the station had not been included in the Erewash Extension bill, so design work and track layouts were started only in April 1861. The following month Thomas Smith of Leicester, who had built the MCR station in that town, was awarded the contract to build the station on a single island platform. This was constructed south of Long Eaton station on the eastern side of the original MCR line, a new southbound 'up' line being constructed around the new station. In September approval was given to build a gas works at Sheet Stores Junction to supply the stores, new station and junction signals and, by the end of the year, the station and the new north and south junctions were almost complete. Eventually all was ready for the opening of the Erewash Valley extension to passengers on 1 May 1862. At the same time the original MCR Long Eaton ('Junction' from 1847) station was closed and in December plans approved for the resiting of 'Toton for Long Eaton' station on the Erewash Valley line a little further south at Tithe Barn Lane where it remained (as Long Eaton) until closure in 1967.

All expresses and local trains stopped at Trent, and Nottingham immediately benefited from an improved London service. In 1852 the fastest trip to the capital took 3hr 45min and the slowest 7hr 20min, with a return service of exactly 4hr or by an exceptionally slow 7pm train from Euston which took 9hr 30min. In 1862 it was possible to reach London (King's Cross) from Nottingham in 3hr 5min and return in exactly 3hr.

Trent station was built in the same MR gothic style as the comparatively new stations on the London extension between Wigston and Bedford. With impressive cast-iron and glass canopies, refreshments rooms and all the other

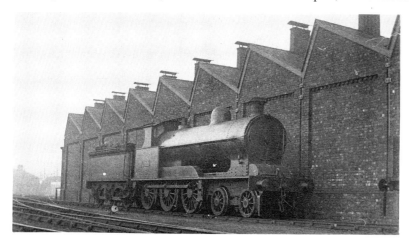

Left:
Another rare view, this time of the LNWR shed at Colwick with LNWR '19in goods' 4-6-0 No 1377 outside. *F. H. Gillford/John Marshall Collection*

25

'modern' facilities, it must have made Nottingham station feel just slightly old-fashioned. Improvements there were squeezed in where possible. Increasing passenger numbers meant that extra booking windows and barriers had to be ordered at the beginning of 1860 and, two years later, the MR agreed to install a cab stand outside the station to alleviate the nuisance of cabs standing on the road. More toilets and a cloakroom were added in 1863 but it wasn't until 1870 after Westcroft Canal, just south of the station, had been filled in any way, that the station could be enlarged in any way. By then there were over 150 trains working through Nottingham most weekdays, of which approaching 80 were passenger trains, but the MR only saw fit to add one extra platform to the south of the station.

This was strangely shortsighted as the company had by then a number of extension schemes that were intended to increase the number of trains passing through the town. In 1866 they had successfully gained Parliamentary approval for a line between Radford, on the Leen Valley line, and Trowell, on the Erewash Valley line, but, although this would have given better access to and from the latter line, it would still have involved north-south trains reversing at Nottingham. Powers to build the connection were allowed to lapse, but revived in 1870 in connection with plans to create a completely new main line south from Nottingham via Melton Mowbray and Manton to Rushton on the London extension.

This stringing together of existing routes to create a new main line was partly in response to traffic needs, and partly to counter the threats posed by a number of new lines promoted by rival companies. The manoeuvring and implications of this assault on the MR's monopoly are discussed in the next chapter, because the true motive for expansion was really the quest for coal and not passengers.

MR Freight Facilities at Nottingham

When the MCR first opened between Nottingham and Derby, goods traffic was apparently very light. The first report of receipts for 'merchandise' appear in the *Railway Times* of 26 October 1839, when £3 6s 7d was made in the week ending 19 October. Early plans of the first station show the goods warehouse adjacent to a short branch cut from the Nottingham Canal into the station yard and, at the time of writing, the bridge carrying the towpath over this branch is still in use.

Once the original MCR station had been superseded in 1848, the site and all the existing buildings were rapidly converted for goods use. At the end of 1849, offices were removed from the old goods warehouse so that it could be used as a grain store. This obviously proved inadequate because in September the following year the tender of G. Thompson of Derby for £7,962 was accepted for the construction of an entirely new corn warehouse and in March 1851 the tender of Cope & Co of Derby for £896 5s was accepted for the installation of a hoist. The old trainshed was then converted for the reception of bar-iron and 'other goods' as a Way & Works minute of 14 July 1852 reports, and an extra goods platform was added the following year.

By 1855 goods traffic was obviously increasing because, in December that year, the Town Council appointed a committee to '...enquire into the evils of the level crossing over Queen's Road...'. It was reported that continual shunting took place over the crossing and, it was implied, that the crossing gates were being closed for perhaps longer than necessary. The Board of Trade ordered that the gates should be kept open to road traffic except for the passage of trains and, at the end of 1857, the railway company installed 'self-acting' gates to try and improve the situation.

As the MR's goods facilities began to grow inexorably between Queen's Road and Mansfield Junction, Wilford Road level crossing also became a problem for the Town Council. This road, like Arkwright Street, was being gradually extended southwards, and the Council introduced a bill in the Parliamentary Session of 1862 for another bridge over the Trent. (Wilford Road bridge over the river opened in June 1870.) In January 1861, it was presented with the MR's plans for a road bridge to replace the level crossing and, after arguments over the width of the carriageway, the Council agreed to contribute £450 in order to ensure it would be 36ft wide. On 31 December 1861, John Palmer was entrusted with building the bridge stonework for £2,960 and, in March the following year, Handyside & Co of Derby secured the contract to supply the ironwork for £2,600. By the end of the year the bridge was complete, but the MR was then faced with compensation claims amounting to £29,684. After negotiation this was reduced to only £5,593!

Although freight traffic was increasing throughout the 1850s and 1860s, the goods facilities at Nottingham were added to only in a seemingly piecemeal fashion with a careful eye kept on economy. Following the removal of the old engine turntable from the goods yard at the beginning of 1864 a more co-ordinated improvement scheme was drawn up but, when the plans were completed and the estimate for implementation costed at £10,000, it seems that they were either abandoned or postponed because piecemeal changes continued as before. Throughout the MR committee minutes, there are references to equipment and even buildings being reused and, as an example of this at the end of 1864, the old weighing machine from Sileby was moved to the Stores Department at Nottingham. New ale stores were planned for the brewers of Burton in September 1865 but, instead of a building erected specifically for the purpose, the MR decided to utilise spare arches under the new Queen's Road bridge when that was finished. Whilst the bridge was under construction in November 1867, temporary arrangements had to be made in the goods yard, and it is uncertain whether the ale stores were ever installed as suggested, because in 1869 plans were drawn up to turn the 1851 engine shed into an ale store.

The building of Queen's Road bridge, or viaduct as it was sometimes referred to at the time, came about after considerable local agitation. In July 1863 a memorial from Nottingham ratepayers to the Town Council painted a colourful picture of the problems encountered at the level crossing: 'In consequence of the widespan of the Railway gates the little warning given and the unseen rapidity with which they are opened, foot passengers and carriages are not infrequently entrapped between them and left to save themselves as best they can from being crushed by Trains rushing past without notice.' The Council set up the inevitable committee, and the MR secured an Act to construct Queen's Road viaduct in 1866. At the same time the company received powers to fill in Westcroft Canal. The tender for bridge construction was awarded to Benton & Woodiwiss of Derby in

August the following year for £10,749 7s 11d but, as with Wilford Road bridge, compensation added to the railway company's final bill. James E. Hall, one of the MR's most successful early contractors, was one who claimed damages and, although the MR refused to pay him the full £2,500 he demanded, they did compensate him with a small piece of land next to the station, plus £1,300.

MR Locomotive Facilities

Locomotive facilities at Nottingham remained modest until the end of the 1860s. In the summer of 1851 plans and estimates were completed for a new engine shed to hold not less than 16 locomotives in the northeast corner of the site occupied by the 1848 station. This semi-circular building with at least 11 lines radiating into it from a turntable was constructed for £3,300 by Neale & Wilson of Grantham who were, at that time, operating the trains between Nottingham and Grantham for the AN&B&EJR. Barely two years later, the original MCR shed was demolished and 'smiths shops' erected on the site.

By 1865, as the number of locomotives allocated to Nottingham had obviously increased, plans were drawn up for larger premises on unoccupied land to the east of Wilford Road. In April 1867 J. E. Hall was given the job of building the new shed for £12,622 15s 2d, the ironwork being provided by Harropp & Summerville for a further £3,000. The new shed survived almost exactly 100 years.

Toton and the Erewash Valley line

Whilst the Erewash Valley line was under construction in 1846, Benjamin Smith of Chesterfield built three new blast furnaces on the site of

Left:
Locomotive Junction in the heart of Colwick yard, looking north from the footbridge over the lines into the LNWR shed behind L. C. E. Shelbourn when he took this photograph in the 1920s. *NCCLSL/3783*

27

the 18th century Stanton ironworks and, although his son on giving evidence to the House of Lords Committee hearings voiced concern that the new railway would not give the company sufficient stimulus to compete with the established Butterley ironworks, it was obviously no coincidence that Smith had chosen to invest in new plant and equipment at exactly the time the Erewash line was nearing completion.

By 1848 the Stanton furnaces were producing 10,400 tons of iron per annum and the three new blast furnaces of the Butterley Co, only a few miles away at Codnor Park, were producing 10,920 tons. Thus, within months of their opening, Stanton and Codnor Park had become two of the most important ironworks in Derbyshire — an achievement entirely due to their position on the Erewash Valley railway line. The Erewash Canal could not have carried enough raw materials to have sustained such an output and, although in 1849 there was still more coal moving by canal than by rail, only four years later that trend had been completely reversed. The canal went into a steady decline from then on. When the MR's main line through Northamptonshire opened in 1857 new markets were immediately opened up for that county's iron ore in Derbyshire — 15,603 tons of iron ore was sent by rail to Stanton in that year alone. One of the reasons for extending the Erewash Valley line through to Clay Cross in 1861 was to ease the supply of Northamptonshire iron ore to the furnaces of northeast Derbyshire, since the quarrying of local ore had declined.

In a very short time the Erewash Valley line had become a very lucrative and vital mineral artery for the MR. In 1856, 867,288 tons of coal was carried by rail from the collieries in the valley and, to deal with this amount of traffic — bearing in mind that contemporary railway wagons would hold little more than six tons each and, therefore, hundreds of them were needed to cope with colliery output — sidings were laid out just south of Stapleford & Sandiacre station at Toton. Toton was initially important for the ballast extracted there on land belonging to Lord Vernon but the first reference to the site for 'the accommodation of goods traffic' occurs in the Way & Works Committee minutes of 2 August 1853 when a short siding was authorised. Vernon's ballast pit was relinquished at the end of 1855, after which time there was a progressive expansion of the sidings.

This expansion was a direct indicator of the rapidly increasing amount of coal mined locally which, fed through to Toton, had to be marshalled into southbound trains. By the end of 1856 there was a turntable at Toton and both horses and locomotives were used for shunting.

In December John Wood's tender of £244 was accepted for the construction of a gas works and, a year later, in November 1857 a siding for crippled wagons was authorised. Early in 1858 Wood was again busy, this time erecting a smithy for the Locomotive Department and 10 railway cottages for £1,000 (rented out for 2s 9d per week).

Extra land was purchased from Richard Birkin in 1861, and an estimate of £5,500 was obtained for the provision of more sidings in August 1869. As accommodation for wagons increased, so too did the complement of locomotives and horses for shunting them. In October 1859 a tender of £168 10s was accepted for additional stables for seven horses and, six years later, plans were drawn up for the stabling of 14 more. This was followed in 1869 by the erection, undertaken by the Derby firm of Eastwood Swingler & Co, of a shed for 24 engines which was to survive until the end of steam in the 1960s.

The Ambergate, Nottingham & Boston & Eastern Junction Railway

Between 1839 and 1850, the MR had a complete monopoly of rail traffic in and around Nottingham. During the 'Railway Mania' it had bought off the independent Nottingham & Mansfield Railway and seen the demise of many other grandiose competitive schemes. But there was one independent local railway company, which having survived the ordeal of 1845, eventually caused the MR to regret not having made a more concerted effort either to foil or absorb its particular scheme.

The Ambergate, Nottingham & Boston & Eastern Junction Railway received the Royal Assent on 16 July 1846 for 90 miles of railway from a junction with the MR at Ambergate via the Leen Valley, through Nottingham courtesy of the MR, on to Grantham and a junction with the GN at Spalding with branches to Sleaford and Boston. The 'Ambergate's' independent route through West Bridgford, which would have connected its eastern and western halves, had been lost during the Parliamentary debates of 1845. As part of a 'friendly' agreement with the MR, the latter agreed to allow the AN&B&EJR to use about four miles of its Leen Valley line west of Nottingham, a route which had received the Royal Assent on the same day as the AN&B&ECR. The Ambergate was also obliged by its Act to purchase the Nottingham and the Nottingham & Grantham canals, which considerably reduced the capital available for railway construction.

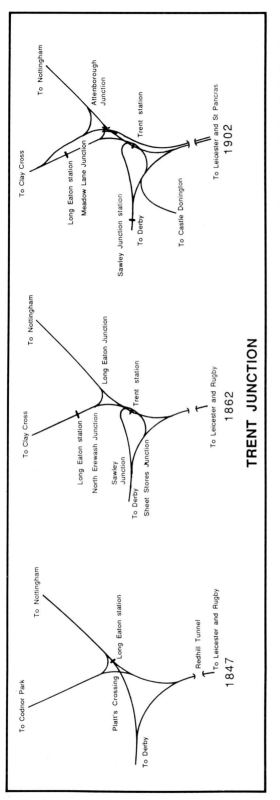

TRENT JUNCTION

To Nottingham
Attenborough Junction
Trent station
To Clay Cross
Long Eaton station
Meadow Lane Junction
Sawley Junction station
To Derby
To Castle Donington
To Leicester and St Pancras
1902

To Nottingham
Long Eaton Junction
Trent station
To Clay Cross
Long Eaton station
North Erewash Junction
Sawley Junction
Sheet Stores Junction
To Derby
To Leicester and Rugby
1862

To Nottingham
Long Eaton station
To Codnor Park
Platt's Crossing
To Derby
Redhill Tunnel
To Leicester and Rugby
1847

Almost immediately the Board was approached by the GN who offered to lease the company, and by the Eastern Counties Railway who offered to purchase it. Understandably, having survived the rigours of steering the bill successfully through Parliament, the AN&B&EJR clung to its independence and, at a special meeting on 8 October, it announced that John Underwood, the principal engineer, had already made a start staking out the line between Colwick and Grantham. It optimistically estimated that completion of this section of the line would be within 12 months with the extension eastwards to Spalding and Boston occupying another eight months. This estimate was obviously based on the 12 months it had taken the MR to complete its 33-mile long Nottingham-Lincoln line, which had opened only two months prior to the Ambergate's announcement. But the company was soon to realise that the building of the MR's line had been uncharacteristically rapid and was not to be repeated with its own line.

A little more realistically the company anticipated that two years would be needed to complete the western section to Ambergate and that this was to be delayed until the completion of the Grantham line. However, problems arose immediately and the following months witnessed considerable changes in plan. Not content with its friendly agreement with the MR, the company proposed in November 1846 an independent terminus of its own in Nottingham just north of the MR's station at the end of a short branch off that company's Leen Valley line. It also revived its plans for a line through West Bridgford, which would have meant crossing the MR on the level at Mansfield Junction. And just south of this crossing, it projected another branch parallel to the MR, across Queen's Road just yards from the MR station, to join the MR west of London Road. Ten days before Christmas, Nottingham Council, already regretting its decision to allow the MR to cross Queen's Road on the level, opposed the Ambergate's intentions to do the same. This forced the company to draw up plans for an expensive viaduct across the Meadows.

In March the following year, the Council gave its approval to the viaduct but, that summer, the AN&B&EJR's West Bridgford line failed once again in Parliament and, with it, went plans for the various branches and separate Nottingham station. Nevertheless, George Wythe of Reigate, who had been awarded the contract to build the Bottesford-Grantham section of the line for £131,728 in March had already made a start at both Bottesford and Gonerby, and between four and five hundred navvies and nearly 50 horses were already at work. Morale was given another boost in July when agreement was reached with the MR for joint stations at Lenton, Radford, Bobbers Mill and Basford and, by August, the line to Boston and Spalding had been staked out. So buoyant was the company that, when the GN made another advance that month, the Directors were unanimous in their rejection of any offer. In November Greaves, Smart & Adams were given the task of completing the line between Colwick and Bottesford and, honouring its agreement of 1846, the MR deposited plans for a connection with the AN&B&EJR at Bulwell on its Leen Valley line to give that company access to Nottingham from the west.

Unfortunately the price of this 'concession' was a crippling contribution of £13,000 from the AN&B&EJR and, although by the beginning of 1848 four and a half miles of permanent way had been laid, the MR payment had obviously depleted limited capital. Extra funds proved almost impossible to secure and, at a special meeting in Nottingham on 19 May 1848, it was reluctantly suggested that the company should drop its plans for extensions beyond Bulwell and Grantham. In August the engineer reported tactfully that '...the works had been prosecuted as vigorously as the state of the company finances would permit...' which meant that completion of the Grantham line was entirely dependent on funding.

The company minutes at this time record many fine arguments as to why the AN&B&EJR should be built in its entirety, but the inevitable had to be faced. In November the AN&B&EJR prepared to drop plans for its most easterly and westerly extensions and, at another special meeting in Nottingham on 19 December, the Board was criticised by a large number of shareholders for not having reached this decision earlier. By January the following year, the timber viaduct at Radcliffe was almost complete but most of the company minutes at this date are taken up with the forfeiting of shares because of the abandonment decision. Eight months later, in August 1849, a call on shares failed to raise sufficient money to finish even the Grantham line, and a long list of people who had not responded to this call took up several pages of the company's minute book. The impressive cast-iron arch to span the River Trent at Radcliffe lay waiting to be positioned as a despondent winter of inactivity followed. It was all very sad.

Finally, in February 1850 with apparently little ceremony, the arch was swung into place — bearing a cast-iron plate with Clayton, Shuttleworth & Co Lincoln, 1850 upon it — and, with only the permanent way across this structure left to complete, the line was ready for traffic. In June the MR agreed to provide the signals and signalman at Colwick Junction, at the expense of the AN&B&EJR of course, and reduced to a rural branch line between Colwick Junction and Grantham, the AN&B&EJR finally opened to the public on 15 July 1850.

Four passenger trains each way were operated on weekdays and two on Sundays between the MR station in Nottingham and Grantham from this date, and the launch of a goods service followed a week later. The fare between the two towns was 5s first-class, 3s 9d second, 1s 11d third and 1s 10¾d fourth-class. The fastest trains took just an hour, and the slowest 1¼hr. But, after the struggles to complete the line, there was room for some fun. David Joy the

Below:
In the yard at Colwick about the time of the Grouping is GN 0-8-2T No 136 with wagons from the Stanton Ironworks. *T. G. Hepburn/Rail Archive Stephenson*

young locomotive superintendent of the line recalled 'People used to come and get on the line at the road crossing gates and wave their umbrellas at us to stop as if we were an old stage-coach...We didn't.'

By 1850 the AN&B&EJR was more amenable to outside assistance and, when the GN once again proposed a working agreement leading to a lease, the AN&B&EJR's directors accepted the terms. An agreement was entered into on 31 March 1852 whereby the GN would work the line as from 1 July that year. This, of course, was timed to coincide with the planned opening of the GN's final section of main line between Peterborough and Retford, via Grantham, when the company could contemplate a Nottingham-London service in direct competition with the MR. Realising this, the MR immediately contested the GN agreement with the Ambergate in Chancery and an injunction was granted preventing its implementation. Nevertheless, the GN advertised through carriages between London and Nottingham and, when the first one arrived in an Ambergate train at the MR's Nottingham station on 2 August 1852, its return was prevented when the GN engine, having detached from the train, was forced into the original MCR engine shed by a number of MR locomotives and the rails taken up. The fight between the London & York Railway and the MR during the 'Railway Mania' was still a bitter memory and, as if a continuation of this battle, a lengthy legal fight then ensued.

The MR accused the GN of infringing the Court of Chancery injunction, but the GN maintained that its captured engine had been hired by the Ambergate company. Despite this, the MR was granted another injunction preventing

any rival companies' locomotives working into its Nottingham station without first being certified by the MR. The GN continued to sell through tickets from Nottingham but the MR prevented through goods and parcels traffic, making the Ambergate cart all such traffic to and from its shed at Colwick.

Not surprisingly, by the end of the year, the Ambergate had plans drawn up for an extension between Colwick and a terminus of its own in Nottingham. The Town Council approved of the new terminus as it challenged the MR's existing monopoly. It also approved of the Ambergate's intention to strengthen its agreement with the GN but minuted its opposition to the Ambergate's thoughts of selling to the MR or LNWR. By May 1853, the MR and GN had reached agreement about their Nottingham traffic but, in September that year, the Town Council noted with approval the House of Commons sanction for the new terminus and the rejection of any sale to the MR or LNWR. However, the bill did not pass through the House of Lords and it was not until 3 July the following year that the Royal Assent was received for the extension. At the end of the same month the agreement with the GN received Parliamentary approval and, in June 1855, the GN finally acquired all the Ambergate's rolling stock, plant and locomotives.

The GN inherited nine engines, all but one built by E. B. Wilson & Co who had contracted to run the Ambergate when it opened. Nos 1 and 2, which were 0-4-0WTs, carried the names *Grantham* and *Rutland* respectively; No 3 was of the same class but unnamed; No 4 was a 2-2-2 built by R. & W. Hawthorn & Co in 1853, and No 5 was also a 2-2-2; Nos 6, 8 and 9 were 0-6-0s, and No 7 a 2-4-0. All were rebuilt by their new owners.

The extension into Nottingham was engineered by John Underwood, built by Adams & Cope, and was finally brought into use on 3 October 1857. To the west of the junction at Colwick the line paralleled the MR for about a mile and then did so again between Meadow Lane and London Road where an impressive new terminus was built in brick with stone dressings to the design of T. C. Hine. An equally impressive warehouse — the top floor of which (suspended from the roof trusses) was devoted to corn — was erected in the goods yard along with a two-road engine shed. Sidings were also laid into the town gas works which was situated on the north of the station site between the yard and the Nottingham Canal.

In May 1860 the company changed its name to the Nottingham & Grantham Railway & Canal Co and a year later the GN successfully negotiated a 999-year lease. The agreement was barely a year old before the GN was looking to extend into the coalfields of the Erewash Valley, the route chosen being almost the same as that abandoned by the AN&B&EJR 10 years earlier. A junction was planned immediately east of London Road station, the line running behind the station and parallel with the Nottingham Canal on a viaduct between London Road and Wilford Road before swinging northwards up the Leen Valley at Lenton, skirting the northern edge of Wollaton Park, close to Awsworth and on to join the MR near the Codnor Park Iron Works. Nottingham Town Council was unhappy about the plans, and the MR immediately entered into negotiations with the GN to give it access to the Notts & Derbyshire coalfield over its lines. In 1863 agreement was reached between the GN, MS&L (who channelled South Yorkshire coal southwards over the GN) and MR on rates to be charged for moving coal to London from South Yorkshire, Notts & Derbyshire, and Leicestershire, and the GN's Codnor Park extension bill was withdrawn.

Two years elapsed before the MR minuted its formal intention to form a junction between the two companies just east of London Road, Nottingham, to facilitate the transfer of coal, and it wasn't until April 1866 that they agreed to joint sidings to be financed equally by each company. Considering the restricted site and the limited capacity of the wagons then available, it is truly remarkable that nearly 82,000 tons of coal taken out from Nottinghamshire collieries by the GN in 1870 were all shunted through these sidings.

Seen from the MR's Nottingham-Lincoln line, between London Road and Trent Lane Junction, an unidentified LNWR 2-4-0 makes a spirited start from the AN&B&EJR station.
T. G. Hepburn/Rail Archive Stephenson

5. 1870-79 Expansion and the Battle for Coal

In the last few years of the 1870s hundreds of men and horses were once again at work in and around Nottingham excavating cuttings, constructing embankments and bridges, as new railway lines seemed to approach the town from all points of the compass. To Nottingham Council, the MR and GN must have appeared more active than they had done for years and, with luck, the town would benefit. But it must have been equally clear that the railway companies' sudden industry was not completely altruistic.

Following a depression in the market for coal in 1867-68, the GN was put under pressure from the MS&L to revise the rates for South Yorkshire traffic as the MR's coal trade had recovered more strongly than the former's, aided by the opening of the MR's own line into London, and the increasing output from the new pits of the Leen Valley, (Hucknall 1 & 2 sunk 1861-62; Annesley sunk in 1865 and Bulwell in 1867). Sir Edward Watkins, already chairman of the MS&L, threatened to promote an independent line southwards, and it was even suggested that coal should be taken by the MS&L to Grimsby and shipped to London instead of travelling over the GN to the capital. Arbitration on the matter only confirmed the terms of the existing Coal Traffic Agreement and so, in 1870, aware that it needed both the MR's co-operation in the Notts & Derbyshire coalfield and the MS&L's traffic but could not please both partners, the GN

decided to reduce its rates. The MR immediately responded by lowering its rates and a tit-for-tat exchange culminated, in April 1871, with the MR abolishing its through rate for Notts & Derbyshire coal travelling to London via Grantham, effectively excluding the GN from the Erewash Valley. Then, despite having defended the MS&L and South Yorkshire coal interests and incurred the wrath of the MR, the GN discovered that plans for a nominally independent line to carry coal between the MS&L near Lincoln and the GE (of which Watkins was also a director) just north of Cambridge was to be introduced into Parliament at the end of the same month. Briefly, and perversely, the MR and GN found themselves on the same side to defeat this MS&L and GE line but, afterwards, all parties went their separate ways and the real war by extensions began.

In the Parliamentary Session of 1872 there were five schemes, all fathered by the coal rates disagreement:

● 1. GN — Derbyshire & North Staffordshire Extension Lines. This was a line starting from a junction with the Nottingham & Grantham Railway at Colwick, passing Gedling and then westwards crossing the MR Leen Valley line at Bulwell on to a junction at Awsworth where a branch was projected up the Erewash Val-

Left:
With the construction of the MR's line to Melton Mowbray, the most important London expresses arrived and departed from the east end of Nottingham station. Here MR 4-4-0 No 325 enters under London Road bridge just before the Grouping.
T. G. Hepburn/Rail Archive Stephenson

Left:
Bestwood Ironworks was established in 1881 and served from both the MR and GN's Leen Valley lines. This 1930s view shows the MR connection. *NCCLSL*

ley to Pinxton, the main line continuing across the River Erewash and the MR's Erewash Valley line on a 500yd-long cast and wrought-iron viaduct to Ilkeston, Derby and junctions with the North Staffordshire Railway at Egginton to give access to Burton upon Trent and Stafford. (The GN's 1862 route to Codnor Park had by this time been claimed by the MR for its Radford-Trowell branch.)

● 2. MS&L — Doncaster & Worksop Railway.

● 3. MS&L — Market Harborough, Worksop & Nottingham Railway. This was a continuation of the above via Ollerton, Farnsfield, Lowdham and Colston Bassett, to join the LNWR at Market Harborough. Nottingham was to be reached by a branch from Cropwell Bishop with a proposed terminal station immediately south of the GN's London Road station, with no physical connection. (These proposals were the first manifestation of Sir Edward Watkin's desire to get the MS&L to London.)

● 4. MR — Nottingham-Rushton line. This was promoted initially to relieve pressure on the existing lines south of Trent by providing an alternative route south for coal.

● 5. MR — Bennerley & Bulwell line. This formed an additional link between the Erewash and Leen valleys north of the Radford to Trowell line.

In addition, a privately promoted line between Newark and Leicester had been adopted by the GN and was submitted in the same Session, part of which competed with the MS&L's Market

Harborough, Worksop and Nottingham line, and was also seen by the MR as a hostile proposal.

The inevitable inter-company manoeuvring and Parliamentary debate which followed reduced and mutilated these six proposals so that only the GN's Derbyshire extension plans remained intact, receiving the Royal Assent on 25 July 1872. The MS&L agreed to give up its 'wonderful scheme' if the MR cut the Manton-Rushton section from its Nottingham-Rushton extension, which it did. This assured that both the MR's Nottingham-Melton Mowbray and Bennerley-Bulwell branches were successfully negotiated through Parliament. The GN's branch between Newark and Leicester encountered opposition from the MR and the foxhunting lobby in the House of Lords, who managed to reduce the plans to a line only as far south as Melton Mowbray. But, despite this, the GN had the sanction it most wanted — an independent line into the Erewash Valley coalfield.

The MR fights back

After the Parliamentary battles of 1872 were over, there was an interesting realignment of the main protagonists ready for the 1873 Session. The MR did not immediately pursue the southern section of its Nottingham-Rushton line but joined forces with the MS&L to revive that company's plans to build a line from Doncaster to Market Harborough. This time the link at Harborough was to be with the MR not the LNWR, and the MS&L's Nottingham branch was not resuscitated.

Market Harborough proved a popular target because the GN, furthering its plans to reach Leicester from the end of its authorised Melton Mowbray branch, joined forces with the LNWR and included a link with that company at Market Harborough. To induce the LNWR into this joint venture, the GN agreed to allow it running powers to Doncaster via Newark, and also via the Derbyshire Extension line into the Notts & Derbyshire coalfield. To facilitate this a branch was to be built between Stathern and what was to become Saxondale Junction, just west of Bingham on the Nottingham-Grantham line.

Obviously both the plans of the MR&MS&L and the GN&LNWR overlapped and, during April and May 1873, the two rival bills were debated by the same House of Commons Committee. The result was that the Committee favoured the GN extending from Melton Mowbray to Leicester, but not to Market Harborough and not with LNWR support, and the Committee extracted the central section of the MR&MS&L line between Retford and Melton Mowbray. The House of Lords then passed the modified GN bill in July but cut back still further the MR/MS&L scheme by amputating the section from Melton Mowbray to Rushton. Mutilated in this way, the bill was withdrawn.

This effectively ended the 'flirtation' between the MR and MS&L, and in the following year the MR sensibly revived its plans for a line between Manton (just a few miles south of Melton Mowbray on the Syston-Peterborough line) and Rushton on the London Extension. The bill was successfully steered through Parliament and gave the MR the opportunity to complete its alternative route between Nottingham and London. At the same time the Royal Assent was obtained for the final section of the GN&LNWR with the agreed running powers to Doncaster, into the GN's London Road station and more importantly into the Notts and Derbyshire coalfield.

The GN's Derbyshire & North Staffordshire Extension Lines

As far as the town of Nottingham was concerned the Derbyshire & North Staffordshire Extension lines brought no direct benefits. The first section of line to be completed for coal traffic was that between Colwick and Pinxton, which opened on 23 August 1875. This described a wide arc four miles north of Nottingham passing through what was still essentially open countryside before turning north up the Erewash Valley. The first station north of Colwick conveniently served Gedling, but the GN was obviously embarrassed about the next one which was at least half a mile from the nearest town. After just a month as 'Bestwood & Arnold', the station was renamed 'Daybrook for Arnold & Bestwood' and finally ended up as just 'Daybrook' after the nearby stream. The next station was originally called 'Dob Park' but it too changed names after only a few months to 'Basford & Bulwell', indicating perhaps that it truly served neither village. Kimberley was bisected and the station conveniently situated, and then there were village stations at Newthorpe & Greasley, Eastwood & Langley Mill, Codnor Park & Selston, and Pinxton.

The initial passenger service consisted of seven weekday trains each way, later increased to nine with three each way on Sundays when the line was completely opened to Pinxton on 1 August 1876. The remainder of the line beyond Awsworth to Derby was opened in 1878, passenger trains between Nottingham and Derby running from 1 April, with nine each way during the week and three on Sundays. The lace and hosiery makers of Ilkeston probably benefited more than others on this final extension as the MR's station at the end of a short branch off

Right:
Newstead Colliery was sunk in 1875 and connected to both the MR and GN's Leen Valley lines.
LMAG&RS/Newton Collection

the Erewash Valley line had closed in 1870 and, since then, would-be passengers had had to use Ilkeston Junction station a mile away on the 'wrong' side of the River Erewash. Responding to the GN invasion, the MR reopened its Ilkeston Town branch and station on 1 July 1879.

But the primary reason for building the line had been to reach coal and, within the triangle of land formed by the Nottingham-Grantham line and the Derbyshire Extension at Colwick, 23 sidings, including 11 down roads for empties and 12 up lines for loaded wagons, were laid out to handle this traffic. At the same time a modest engine shed was built with four roads under two pitched roofs, and eight GN trains of empties served the local collieries daily, the loaded trains being dispatched from Colwick to New England, Peterborough and various other centres.

The GN & LNWR

Under construction at the same time as the Derbyshire Extension lines was the GN&LNWR. It was opened in stages, the purely GN section between Newark and Bottesford Junction on the Nottingham-Grantham line opening for goods trains in April 1878, and to passengers from 1 July. The GN immediately used this as an opportunity to compete with the MR for traffic between Nottingham and Newark, and they started with a passenger service of six trains each way on weekdays and one return journey on Sundays.

Earlier that year the GN had decided to build a station with a central island platform on the western tip of the Colwick triangle, according to official company minutes, so that passengers could change trains without going into Nottingham, and 'for the use of trains of the LNWR when the joint lines are completed'. The station was built but, at the beginning of 1879, it was agreed to provide extra platform accommodation at the London Road terminus, Nottingham, for the LNWR. This was probably complete by 15 December that year when the Joint line between Saxondale Junction, on the Nottingham-Grantham line, and Stathern Junction, along with the rest of the line between Bottesford Junction and Welham (just north of Market Harborough), was opened. A passenger service of four trains each way was started between Nottingham London Road and Market Harborough. The GN and LNWR shared the workings, with the GN running on to Northampton. The purely GN branch from Marefield to Leicester opened on 15 May 1882. There appear to have been no booked passenger trains between Leicester and Nottingham, and regular services concentrated on runs between Nottingham and Market Harborough, between Nottingham and Newark, and services from Leicester to Grantham.

With the opening of the GN's Derbyshire extension, and the GN&LNWR within months of each other, Nottingham London Road station suddenly became very busy. By 1879 there were nearly 80 passenger trains into and out of the station every weekday with a number of extra services on Saturdays. Activity also increased at Colwick, where the LNWR built its own eight-road engine shed a little to the south of the GN one in 1879-80. The company benefited considerably through its partnership with the GN, not only gaining access to the Notts & Derbyshire coalfield, once the Joint line through Leicestershire was opened, but also to the South Yorkshire coalfield. The company took full advantage of its running powers via Newark, and vast quantities of South Yorkshire coal passed through that town before World War 1.

The MR's Bennerley-Basford line

By the time the Act was received for this line in 1872 there was already a triangular junction at Bennerley Junction with a branch serving Bennerley Colliery (which was to become the site of the Awsworth Iron Co blast furnaces), as well as Digby and Speedwell collieries (sunk in 1866 and 1869 respectively). Construction of the new through line to Basford and the Leen Valley was entrusted to T. Oliver from Horsham, and work began in the spring of 1875. The first section from Basford to a point just northeast of Kimberley, where a branch turned due north to Watnall colliery, was opened on 3 December 1877. The rest of the line didn't open until 12 August 1879 and, although stations appear to have been completed by then, booked passenger trains did not start for another three years.

The MR's Radford Junction-Trowell Junction and Nottingham-Rushton lines

Although Nottingham Town Council had supported the GN Derbyshire extension, GN&LNWR lines and the MR's Nottingham-Rushton extension, it was the latter which brought the most noticeable benefits to the town in the 1880s by placing Nottingham on a through main line for the first time. A vital part of this new route was the connection between Radford, on the Leen Valley line, and Trowell, on the Erewash Valley line, which opened to passenger traffic on 1 May 1875. At Radford Junction the Leen Valley tracks were realigned further west so that Ilkeston Road could be carried over the railway on a bridge and a new station constructed upon it. Just around the corner from the junction the Nottingham Mineral Railway was crossed on the level by the new line at Babbington Crossing.

Leaving the Nottingham-Lincoln line just east of London Road bridge and curving away southwards to cross the Trent on a simple but handsome three-span bow-string bridge, the Nottingham-Melton Mowbray line was opened for goods traffic on 1 November 1879. One of the engineers of the line immediately south of Nottingham was Edward Parry. He remained closely associated with railways in the town becoming resident engineer for the MS&L's extension between Annesley and East Leake 20 years later.

Finally, mention must be made of the MR's extension of its Leen Valley line from Mansfield to Shireoaks Junction, a point on the MS&L just west of Worksop, opened to passengers on 1 June 1875 and providing Nottingham with a rail link to Worksop and Retford where the MR established goods facilities.

MR freight facilities

Major investment in Nottingham's goods facilities also dates from the 1870s after Queen's Road bridge had been completed, and this decade began to produce some of the buildings and yard layouts that were to remain virtually unaltered for the next 100 years.

In October 1872 plans were finalised for the stabling of 51 horses, with wheelwrights and smiths' shops, mess room and straw shed, and the following month J. E. Hall's tender of £3,983 14s 6d was accepted for this work. At the end of the year, just in time for Christmas, he was also entrusted with the installation of a new timber yard but in September 1873 it was the rival firm of W. & H. Harris which was awarded the prestigious job of building a completely new 'goods office' (at a price of £4,842 15s 9d) on the site of the original MCR station which was to be demolished. (The replacement building still stands on Carrington Street and has been recently cleaned externally.)

Only two months later another very remunerative contract was awarded for a large new Bonded Stores between Queen's Road and Mansfield Junction, plans of which had been drawn up in May 1872. J. & E. Wood's tender of £9,936 10s 3d was accepted on 4 November; the following May Eastwood Swingler & Co of Derby received the contract to supply ironwork for £1,424 0s 1d, and in June was contacted to supply further amounts for £4,070 18s 6d. At the opposite end of the station, improvements followed for horse, fish and parcels traffic which involved the widening of London Road bridge, the contract for supplying the iron girders being awarded to Eastwood Swingler & Co in November 1876.

By 1877 there were over 200 passenger and goods trains working through Nottingham, and many more coal trains emanating from the Leen and Erewash valleys. The first very obvious indicator of this traffic growth occurred in July 1874 when new up and down goods lines were brought into use between the south of Redhill tunnel and Leicester. This was followed shortly afterwards by the establishment of extensive new sidings just east of Beeston station. In August 1872 authority had been sought for the purchase of 43¼ acres of land between Lenton and Beeston and, 14 months later the first plans and estimates were put forward for 'sorting sidings' and wagon shops on this land. The initial purchase did not go ahead and, in May 1874, the MR revised its plans agreeing to acquire 64¼ acres of land for £30,300. Sidings were laid sometime after this and, on 19 March 1877, the yard began to deal with mineral trains running from a new connection at Cinderhill Colliery. In the same year the MR turned its attention to the building of a creosoting works at Beeston; the tender from Cowan Sheldon & Co for £1,771 being accepted in July for the necessary machinery.

Extra sidings and more goods and passenger trains to work meant more locomotives had to be stationed locally. Accommodation at Toton was doubled early in the decade by the provision of another shed for 24 locomotives, both this and the original structure, although square in plan, having central 42ft diameter turntables with radiating tracks. At the same time new lodging accommodation was provided for drivers for £1,859 16s 8d and 40 cottages were erected for other employees at a cost of £6,392 9s 8d. Forty-seven more were added in 1873, some of these terraced houses being situated on the east side of the main line which ran through the centre of the complex at Toton.

Locomotive accommodation at Nottingham was dealt with a little later when a large new engine shed was constructed by John Garlick at the beginning of 1876-77 for £17,390 14s 9d. This brought the official locomotive stabling capacity up to 48 engines, a high-level coal stage being erected at the same time along with a seven-road fitting shop with associated wagon turntables provided behind the 1868 shed.

Signalling

Another development during the 1870s, which is commonly regarded as a response to the demand for greater safety, but which was as much a solution to the problems caused by increasing traffic and poor line capacity, was the spread of the block system in and around Nottingham. The telegraph was already in operation on both the MR and GN — an early circuit being authorised between Nottingham and Keyworth in April 1861 with extensions requested between Long Eaton and Wilford Road bridge at the beginning of 1864 and between Mansfield Junction and Queen's Road a year later in anticipation of the opening of new passenger lines there. The first MR 'signalmen's boxes' mentioned as such appeared at the end of 1867 when E. Dunsantoy's tender of a mere £41 2s was accepted for structures at Trent and Langley Mill. This was followed in May 1868 by the decision to introduce the block system between Sheet Stores Junction, Trent Junction and Trent Station South Junction, '...so as to ensure the safety of engines whilst taking water'. At the end of that year the MR authorised single stroke bells for Queen's Road 'junction', London Road, and the junction with the GN to help regulate trains, but these were probably not installed until early 1871, a year after the MR had agreed to push ahead with the introduction of block working between Nottingham, Trent, Wigston Junction and Bedford. It was at this time that the familiar standard MR signalboxes began to appear, one such 'block station' being planned in August 1870 along with a siding at Radcliffe just south of Redhill tunnel.

On the GN the block system first appeared locally between Nottingham and Gonerby tunnel, and on the Derbyshire Extension line in 1875. The latter was equipped from the outset (by McKenzie & Holland of Worcester) with what were to become the company's distinctive signalboxes with decorative barge-boards. By the close of the 1870s both the MR and the GN had evolved many of the operating practices, rules and regulations which were to remain in force for nearly 100 years.

Left:
From 1889 the GN's London Road station also played host to Nottingham Suburban Railway trains, the latter's line running from Trent Lane Junction to Daybrook station, seen here on 6 May 1960. *John Marshall*

6. 1880-93 The Boom Years

By the end of 1879, 839,607 passengers had been booked at Nottingham MR station, earning the company £80,580 in ticket revenue. If miscellaneous parcels and other luggage is added to this figure, the total coaching receipts were just £54 short of £100,000. By 1882 the number of passengers booked had risen to 1,027,777, receipts from tickets to £100,541 and total coaching receipts to £121,744. This healthy upturn in business was in no small part due to the opening to passengers of the MR's Nottingham-Melton Mowbray line on 2 February 1880 followed four months later by the introduction of a new London-Leeds service over the complete line via Kettering (Glendon Junction) and Manton.

Concentrating its London-Leeds/Bradford trains on the new route, with London-Manchester/Liverpool trains running via Leicester, the MR was able to offer Nottingham a considerably faster London service than hitherto. The fastest up journey in 1877 was the 5.00am 'Scotch Express' which took exactly three hours to reach St Pancras, with two returning down services at 10.00am and 10.30am taking 3hr 5min. Via the Manton route, Nottingham and London were only 2hr 40min apart by five up and three down trains, with the 10.00am from St Pancras covering the ground in just 2hr 35min. By these same trains Leeds was only 2hr 5min away from Nottingham.

Expansion in the Erewash and Leen valleys

On 1 September 1882 passenger trains began to run over the MR's line between Bennerley and Bulwell. Stations were provided at Watnall and Kimberley, the latter less than a quarter of a mile from the GN station on that company's Derbyshire Extension line.

This unnecessary, but seemingly inevitable duplication of passenger facilities resulting from the extensions of rival railway companies, was particularly noticeable when the GN pushed its way into the Leen Valley. Having successfully extended into the neighbouring Erewash Valley, the GN rather belatedly turned its attention to the Leen Valley after representations from the colliery owners there. With some speed a line was surveyed, plans deposited for the Parliamentary Session of 1880, and the bill successfully passed on 6 August that year. Within 12 months the new line was carrying coal from Westwood Colliery and, by the end of October 1881, a double line, snaking its way around the existing MR line and barely losing sight of its rival, was in full operation between Leen Valley Junction on the Derbyshire Extension line and Annesley Colliery. Sidings or longer branches served the collieries of Hucknall No 1 and No 2 (sunk 1861-62), Linby (sunk in 1873), Newstead (sunk in 1875) and Bestwood (sunk 1871-72), all of which were already served by the MR.

Passenger stations were provided at Newstead, Linby, Hucknall, Butler's Hill and Bestwood, (Bulwell Forest opening on 1 October 1887). The first three named were only a few hundred yards away from their counterparts of the same name on the MR's line. A service of 12 trains each way and two on Sundays was introduced. It is sufficient to note that it took 40min to reach Nottingham from Linby via the GN and only 30min via the MR.

But it was revenue from mineral traffic that justified the GN's investment in providing a duplicate railway through the Leen Valley. At Bestwood, for example, the arrival of the GN encouraged the colliery company to erect an ironworks next to its coal mine. The new railway connection ran directly off the Leen Valley line, separate from the colliery branch, and the first two blast furnaces were erected parallel to the MR's branch to the colliery at the end of 1881. Both furnaces were operational by March 1882 and remained in blast for the next five years before being joined by another erected between September and December 1887 and put into use the following summer. All three remained operational until the spring of 1890 when one was blown out whilst a new structure was being built. By the following year this was in blast and by December 1891 all four were producing pig iron, the works having doubled in size in just 10 years. They were the first, and remained the only, blast furnaces in Nottinghamshire.

The GN also looked for the same sort of successful intervention in the Erewash Valley. Just as its Leen Valley line was opening to traffic, the company projected a branch off the Derbyshire Extension from Ilkeston (Stanton Junction) south to Ilkeston Colliery, Trowell Ironworks and to the Stanton Ironworks' Hallam Field furnaces (which were built between 1872 and 1874). The five blast furnaces there had doubled the capacity of the Stanton works and reinforced the company's position as one of the most important ironworks in Derbyshire. By comparison the Trowell Ironworks was a much smaller and speculative affair. It had been established by David New at the end of the 1870s to produce a variety of iron fabrications and was situated to the west of the MR's Erewash Valley line with a connection directly opposite Trowell Junction. Looking at OS map evidence it is obvious that the GN also intended to extend its 'Stanton branch' to the Erewash Valley Furnaces (also connected to the MR's Erewash Valley line) just

a few hundred yards north of the Trowell works. However, by the time the GN branch to Stanton's was opened in September 1883, the Erewash Valley Furnace Co was in trouble and, in 1885, its four furnaces went out of blast, remaining inactive until 1898. During the same period the Trowell Works also closed down and, consequently, the GN never extended to either site. Instead, a single line from Stanton Junction north to Nutbrook Colliery was opened on 7 June 1886 and later extended to Heanor in 1891.

The Stanton company remained an important customer for both the MR and the GN throughout their independent existence. The railway companies served the firm's collieries west of Mansfield at Teversal (1869), Pleasley (1877) and Silver Hill (1878) and transported all the coke produced at its ovens established in 1881 at Teversal and Silver Hill. The company also had iron ore quarries at Woolsthorpe, Lincolnshire, connected to the GN via Belvoir Junc-

tion on the Nottingham-Grantham line, and quarries at Wartnaby near Melton Mowbray on the MR. Throughout the 1880s and early 1890s the Stanton Ironworks Co always had either seven or eight furnaces in blast, remaining competitive by gradually diversifying its output from pig iron into the production of cast-iron pipes and, from the early 1890s, cast-iron tube segments for London's deep underground railways.

By comparison, other ironworks in the Erewash Valley traded badly during this period. At the Butterley Co's Codnor Park Works the three blast furnaces there remained out of action for most of the decade. The Erewash Valley Iron Co's plight has already been noted. The situation was better at the Awsworth Iron Co a few miles away at the MR's Bennerley Junction, where all three blast furnaces remained operational between 1880 and 1886. Nevertheless, they had all succumbed by June 1886. Two years later the company was taken over by E. P. Davis, (who also owned the inactive Erewash Furnaces), and although he had all three in blast again by the end of 1889, only two remained so into the 1890s. (By then the works were being referred to as the Bennerley Furnaces.)

But despite the perilous state of these ironworks, it is quite obvious that during the 1880s and early 1890s, both the MR and GN were transporting vast amounts of coal and iron from the Erewash and Leen valleys, as well as fulfilling an increasing demand from the Stanton Ironworks and the Bestwood Iron & Coal companies for iron ore, limestone and coking coal. The tremendous amount of mineral traffic handled by the railways can be gauged by the 941,832 tons of Northamptonshire iron ore transported by the MR into Derbyshire in 1881, and the

1,150,997 tons of minerals handled at Colwick by the GN in 1887.

In 1884 siding accommodation at Colwick had been increased and a new engine shed for 50 locomotives and associated workshops completed by E. Wood at a cost of £11,310. The following year plans were approved by Parliament for a large-scale remodelling of the yard in association with the laying of new up and down goods lines between Saxondale Junction and Radcliffe on the Nottingham-Grantham line. Work began in the spring of 1888 involving complete realignment of the passenger lines between Colwick North and their connection with the Nottingham-Grantham line just east of the bridge over the Trent. New sidings and additional up and down goods lines were laid at the same time. A new signalbox, named Rectory Junction near the Trent bridge, and a new Colwick North box were brought into use in November. J. E. Edwards was awarded the contract to build a new road bridge in place of the station level crossing (Meadow Road) at the beginning of 1889, and the new goods lines between Saxondale and Radcliffe were ready by August 1890. On 23 November the following year Colwick yard's gravity grid iron sidings were ready for traffic.

At the same time a distinct new settlement was developing at Netherfield adjacent to Colwick yard. Between 1880 and 1900 a number of new streets of terraced houses were laid out, whilst the Baptists, Free United and Primitive Methodists all built chapels in this period. The Church of England was represented when St George's church was erected in 1887 on Netherfield Lane (later renamed Victoria Road).

As Colwick yard expanded, so too did the complex at Toton. At the end of March 1881 the

41

general goods yard was closed and its functions transferred to Long Eaton where a new public yard was opened. This allowed Toton to concentrate almost exclusively on heavy mineral traffic and, by 1884, the yard was handling almost 18,000 wagons a month during the summer and nearly 26,000 in the winter, in 16 sorting sidings and nine reception lines on the up side for loaded wagons, and 17 sorting sidings and five reception roads on the down side for empties. The quantity of coal travelling along the Erewash Valley line, marshalled at Toton and then threading its way southwards through the junctions at Trent, combined with iron ore travelling in the opposite direction forced the MR to lay separate goods lines at various places along the Erewash line and, in 1892, it began construction of another double line bridge across the Trent and a new tunnel under Redhill. The contract for the latter work was awarded to Henry Lovatt of Wolverhampton who successfully finished the bridge and tunnel, the latter a mirror image of its MCR counterpart, for £4,152 13s 11d less than his tender price of £52,258 8s 4d. The new goods lines were opened on 13 August 1893.

Right:
At the turn of the century, Toton marshalling yard was converted for hump shunting, and this is the down side as recorded by the official MR photographer on 10 February 1908. *Crown Copyright, courtesy National Railway Museum/DY8873*

Below:
The northern side of the MR Goods & Grain Warehouse showing the connection to the Nottingham Canal, recorded by the official company photographer on 27 March 1922. *Crown Copyright, courtesy National Railway Museum/DY12460*

Nottingham

During these years of industrial and railway expansion, Nottingham was physically and institutionally evolving into a city. The Borough had been successfully enlarged by an Act of Parliament on 11 June 1877, despite both the MR and GN presenting petitions against the bill. The town's new boundaries embraced Lenton, Radford, Basford and Bulwell, Carrington, Sherwood, and Sneinton. The Corporation was keen to assimilate these communities as soon as possible and, in line with other large Victorian manufacturing towns in this period, it was determined to improve the urban environment. Civic pride was immediately manifest in the refurbishment of the Castle as a museum to the designs of T. C. Hine, opened on 3 July 1878 by the Prince and Princess of Wales, and by the building of Nottingham's tree-lined 'Boulevards', Gregory, Radford, Lenton and Castle, in the early 1880s. Then, in 1885, the Borough Engineer, A. Brown, designed the town's impressive new cattle market which was constructed at a cost of nearly £23,000 in Eastcroft with sidings laid directly into the site from the MR.

Only a few hundred yards away, there were considerable alterations at the GN's London Road station. In 1879 it had been agreed to provide additional cover for the platform on the south side of the station apparently used, or to be used by LNWR trains, and in June 1881 £7,816 was allocated for further improvements which judging by the sum of money involved, probably included this new platform awning complete with decorative cast-iron supports and a two-storey building at the south end of the station. At the end of the year Saxby & Farmer received the contract to build the station's new signalbox for £494 2s 8d, and in April 1883 S. & W. Pattinson was awarded a contract for various station improvements which included a new refreshment room. Then, in June the following year, the same company's tender of £3,191 8s 5d was accepted for an extension of the train shed, an addition that can still be clearly seen today at the east end of the station.

In 1884, the LNWR added to the list of bills presented in the Parliamentary Session of that year with particular relevance to the town, by seeking powers to construct its own goods station. Having entered Nottingham through running powers over the GN, the LNWR began work in 1886 on a short branch of its own from Trent Lane Junction across Sneinton Hermitage to a five-acre site just below St Stephen's church. The company must have been very confident of a healthy financial return from its new yard, because the whole site had to be excavated from solid sandstone, and the final cost of construction was in the region of £50,000. The rock was removed by shot blasting and with it disappeared a number of interesting rock houses. When the local *Evening Post* reported on the excavations in May 1887, 120 men were still laboriously removing large quantities of sandstone.

The Manvers Street yard complete with warehouse, signalbox, 12 sidings, and cattle pens, was eventually brought into use on 2 July 1888. The initial daily service consisted of three trains into and four out of the yard, and the LNWR advertised express goods services between Nottingham, London, Liverpool, Manchester and Birmingham. The company also offered a collection and delivery service from Basford, Beeston, Carrington, Colwick, Lenton, Netherfield, Radford, Sherwood and West Bridgford.

Industrially, the 1880s and 1890s witnessed the steady growth of what were to become some of Nottingham's major employers in the 20th century. By 1889 John Player was employing 250 people making cigarettes in his Radford factories, this number increasing to 1,000 by 1898. In 1886 the Humber, Marriott & Cooper Cycle Co of Beeston became a limited company and, in 1892, as Nottingham's largest cycle manufacturer made a £29,663 profit. At the same time Woodhead, Anglois & Ellis of Raleigh Street was also creating a market for its cycles and, in 1896, built a factory for 850 people which was reputed to be the largest cycle factory in the world at the time. Following the rapid expansion of his small business in Goose Gate, Jesse Boot created Boots Cash Chemists in 1883 and, five years later, began to manufacture his own products as the Boots Pure Drug Co.

Nevertheless the two staple industries of hosiery and lace manufacture continued to flourish in and around the town, there being over 80 hosiery and nearly 300 lace manufacturers in Nottingham by 1877, not to mention those in the satellite villages, the numerous independent lace machine holders, merchants and dealers. In May 1883 so great was the quantity of material being dispatched by horse-drawn vehicles from the factories in the congested Lace Market to Nottingham's main railway stations that the town's lace manufacturers and railway carriers petitioned the Corporation for the widening of streets in the area. Due to the problems of cartage through these narrow streets, movement was concentrated on Thursdays, Nottingham's early closing day. The MR station handled an average of 30,000 parcels of lace and millinery a month, a figure that could rise to 5,000 a day for three consecutive days at Christmas. The company boasted that within four hours of receipt from the manufacturer, parcels destined for export via Liverpool would be at the dockside. This specialist traffic was extremely lucrative, because the boxes were classified as 'frail trade', and charged 50% more than ordinary parcels.

At the other end of the spectrum, goods traffic at Nottingham might not be so frail and was sometimes more trouble than it was worth, as the MR's chief clerk discovered when he had to tackle an angry gorilla which escaped from a train in Nottingham station.

Nottingham Central Station

During the 1880s, Nottingham Corporation was very keen to improve the town's main railway facilities particularly for passengers, councillors feeling they were no longer appropriate for a thriving town like Nottingham. The Corporation had been disappointed that the GN's Derbyshire Extension had so obviously avoided the town centre, especially as the same line had cut through the heart of Derby and given that town a new central station. The MR line to Melton Mowbray and Glendon Junction had improved the passenger service to and from London, but it had also emphasised the inadequacy of the MR's 1848 station. So, in October 1881, the General Purposes Committee of the Corporation resolved: 'That....it is desirable that, in the interests of the town, there should be a joint Central Railway Station, and that it is the duty of the Council to facilitate any proceedings which may be taken for the purposes of establishing such station.'

A memorial was sent to the MR, GN and LNWR including a plan drawn up in September by the County Surveyor, Edward Parry, and his assistant, J. Greenhalgh Walker, indicating a 10-acre site designated a few hundred yards north of the Market Place. Part of this area had already been declared unhealthy by the Borough Medical Officer and, therefore, construction of any new station would also facilitate slum clearance. Lower Parliament Street and a section of Upper Parliament Street would be realigned, the railway running due west to east with the station lying between the Theatre Royal and Cranbrook Street (then named Coalpit Lane). Connecting lines were proposed from the MR's Trent bridge in Eastcroft, due north on a viaduct over the MR and GN, through a tunnel under Sneinton Hermitage to join a new branch coming in from the east through a tunnel off the GN's Grantham line and the MR's Lincoln line. Between there and the new station the line would run on a viaduct crossing Manvers Street and Southwell Road amongst others. Exiting from the station to the west, a new line would tunnel under Wollaton Street to join the MR at Radford Junction, whilst another branch also in a tunnel would pass under the northeast corner of the general cemetery, under the Forest Recreation Ground where a station for Hyson Green and the Race Course was proposed, before running due north to join the GN's Leen Valley line half a mile south of the future site of its Bulwell Forest station.

This linking together of all the major routes approaching Nottingham was a sensible and carefully considered project and, given sufficient goodwill and support from all the railway companies concerned, would undoubtedly have benefited the town. Unfortunately competition and not co-operation was the order of the day.

Like all unrealised projects, it seems fanciful now, but there can be little doubt that as Victoria station was eventually built only a few hun-

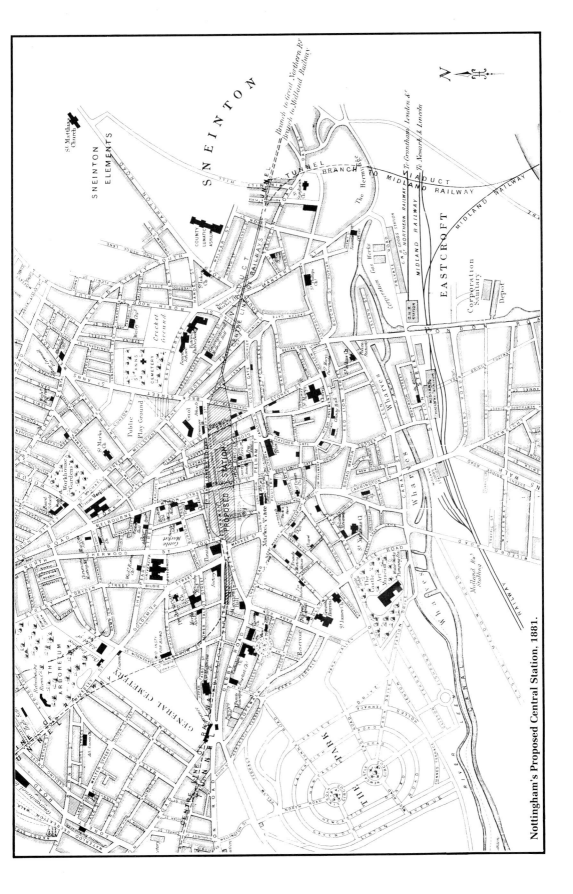

Nottingham's Proposed Central Station, 1881.

dred yards from this proposed site, although on a north-south axis, these Corporation plans must have encouraged the MS&L in its projected London Extension through the heart of Nottingham and also influenced the location of its station. Perhaps, without Corporation pressure for a central station, the MS&L might have been persuaded to construct a more useful interchange station where its new line crossed the MR station?

Urban and suburban transport

This desire for better railway facilities within the town also led the Corporation to support both urban and suburban transport projects. After 1877 it was particularly keen to improve urban transport in order to weld together the communities recently embraced by boundary changes. In 1878 the first sections of horse-drawn tramway were opened between St Peter's Square via Carrington Street to Trent Bridge, and via Station Street to London Road. The new service was operated by the Nottingham & District Tramway Co Ltd. The network was expanded soon afterwards from the Market Place to Basford along Derby, Alfreton and Radford roads, and then along Mansfield Road to Carrington, the two routes being linked via Forest Road.

In 1884 a steam tram was experimentally tried on the Basford route but, until electrification in the early 20th century established the tram as the best answer to urban transport problems, some local businessmen turned their attention to the creation of a suburban railway.

Edward Parry and Walker were involved again, but their plans for the Nottingham Suburban Railway put to the Parliamentary Session of 1886 did not obviously serve any existing suburb. As already noted, Nottingham was expanding at the time and perhaps a new line to the northeast of the town might have encouraged housing development but, being completely cynical about the project, it could be argued with some justification that the main beneficiaries were Parry himself as a director of the Nottingham Patent Brick Co whose works at Thorneywood just happened to be on the route of the new line, and Robert Mellors the leading promoter of the Suburban Railway, who was chairman of the same brick company. Nevertheless, or perhaps because of its involvement, the Corporation backed the project and an agreement with the GN was reached whereby it would work the line, supply the rolling stock and machinery, and have the option to buy the line after 10 years.

The Royal Assent was received on 25 June 1886 for a line between a junction with the GN at Trent Lane, almost due north, to a junction with the same company at Daybrook. Stations were to be built in what was still countryside at Thorneywood, St Ann's Well and Sherwood, as well as a siding to the Nottingham Patent Brick Co works. Only 3¾ miles long, the course of the line was a very difficult one including four tunnels totalling almost ¾ mile. After modifications to the planned junction at Trent Lane in 1887 involving the bridging of the MR's Lincoln line, further complications were forced on the company when the GN insisted on a bridge to take the southbound (up) line across the Grantham line nearby to avoid conflicting train movements.

Work started at Sherwood tunnel in June 1887, and the line was completed by October 1889. Every aspect of the line was constructed to the highest standards and had all the hallmarks of a modern GN line. The typical GN-style signalboxes controlled their equally distinctive somersault signals; each station had substantial brick buildings, the platform structures incorporating decorative canopies, and a wrought-iron footbridge connected each platform.

The line was formally opened on 2 December 1889 with a service of 10 northbound and nine southbound trains. Four of these each way continued along the GN's Leen Valley line to serve Newstead, and connections to and from Derby and Pinxton on the GN's Erewash line were made at Daybrook.

No other attempt was made to build a suburban line within the town, partly because the Nottingham Suburban Railway had proved so costly to construct (£262,500) and partly because only a dozen years after it had opened, Nottingham's commuting population was being well catered for by the Corporation's expanding electric tram network. All the major railway companies failed to rise to this challenge, the most obvious example being the MR's failure to build a station for West Bridgford which was never connected to the tram network but with a population of 2,600 and Urban District status by 1891, was a true Victorian suburb.

Planning the Great Central Railway

In November 1888 Nottingham Corporation set up another committee to further the cause of the Central Station. At the same time the MS&L was depositing its plans to extend southwards from Beighton near Sheffield to join the GN Leen Valley line at Annesley. From there they sought running powers into the Notts & Derbyshire coalfield and into Nottingham London Road station. With hindsight we know that Annesley became the point whence the MS&L began its new main line southwards to Marylebone but, in 1889, the fear was the MS&L extending southwards from the GN at Nottingham. For this reason the GN at first opposed the bill, only withdrawing its opposition when the MS&L gave its assurance that no extension was planned.

The Beighton-Annesley Extension received its Act in 1889 but, by then, the MS&L's assurance was worthless. For the Parliamentary Session of 1891 Sir Edward Watkins revealed his intentions to reach London from Annesley, including a central station in Nottingham close to the Corporation's own preferred site. It is recorded that Watkins was keen to involve any other railway company that might be interested in the new Nottingham station, if they helped share the costs. But none were prepared to see the benefits of this, blinded by their dislike of the man and his maverick challenges to the *status quo*. The MR Board were particularly dis-

dainful and, commenting on a similar idea Watkins had for a central station in Leicester, replied that they regarded both suggestions: '...rather as a move on your Parliamentary Chess Board than as a proposal intended to be seriously considered by practical men acquainted with the conditions and difficulties attending the construction and working of [such] stations...'

The GN who had been invited to help construct and operate the new line, also declined to get involved and, to the relief of apparently everyone, the MS&L London Extension bill was defeated at the committee stage in June 1891.

But despite this failure it was obvious that the company was determined to continue and reintroduce the bill the following year. Realising this the GN reached agreement with the latter for running powers north of Nottingham over the proposed new line and an option to take a half share in the central station. The route through the heart of Nottingham remained unaltered, and Nottingham Corporation having already given its support to the initial MS&L bill did so again. The Beighton-Annesley Extension opened to goods on 24 October1892 and for passengers on 2 January the following year, when the company began to run six trains a day (two on Sundays) over the Suburban and GN Leen Valley line between Sheffield and Nottingham London Road. On 28 March 1893 the MS&L's London Extension bill of 1892 received the Royal Assent.

Below:
The MR's 1896 Goods & Grain Warehouse, with the 1873/74 Goods Office behind fronting Carrington Street, as photographed by the Surrey Flying Services, Croydon c1927. *NCCLSL*

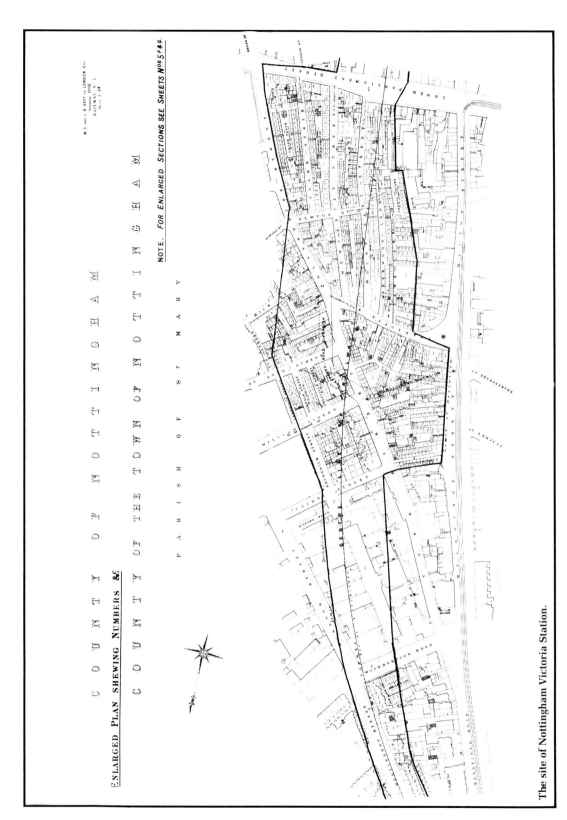

ENLARGED PLAN SHEWING NUMBERS &c.

COUNTY OF NOTTINGHAM

COUNTY OF THE TOWN OF NOTTINGHAM

PARISH OF ST MARY

NOTE. FOR ENLARGED SECTIONS SEE SHEETS Nos 5, F & G.

The site of Nottingham Victoria Station.

7. 1894-1920 The Local Network at its Peak

There is little doubt that the railways throughout Britain reached their peak of efficiency and usefulness in the 20 years leading up to World War 1. The quality and extent of the service during this period has never been matched. For Nottingham businessmen the railways were indispensable arteries taking goods and parcels to anywhere in the world. For the ordinary workers it was a period of unrestricted mobility, with a choice of trams, omnibuses and local trains to and from work, and with the gradual introduction of half-day closing and factory holidays, a chance to get to the seaside, or the Lake District, or practically anywhere else in the country. Railways were a good thing and, during this period, large sums of money were spent on expanding and improving their facilities.

The Great Central Railway

Seven tenders were received in September 1894 for construction of the MS&L extension between Annesley and East Leake (contract No 1). Although Logan & Hemingway's price of £684,451 was not the lowest, the board decided to award the contract to that firm as it already had considerable plant and equipment in the area after having successfully finished the construction of the MS&L extension from Beighton to Annesley. Edward Parry was appointed as the resident engineer for contract No 1, and there is no doubt that he must have been very pleased

and proud to be able to give Nottingham the central station he had planned for in 1881.

Logan & Hemingway began work immediately before winter set in, fencing the route, sinking shafts for Sherwood Rise Tunnel just south of the site for New Basford station, demolishing properties in the Meadows area of Nottingham (which went on into the summer of 1895) and building a temporary bridge over the River Trent. Access for materials north of Nottingham was via the MS&L at Annesley and a connection with the MR at Bulwell. To the south, arrangements were made to use the sidings of Clifton Colliery (sunk 1868-69) themselves connected to the MR at Lenton South Junction. Extremely heavy frosts then slowed progress until the end of March 1895 which confined work to Sherwood Rise and Mansfield Road tunnels. C. R. Hemingway recorded that the excavation of these tunnels was easy, but in comparison work in Victoria Street Tunnel in Nottingham had to proceed very carefully due to the buildings above, and there was massive disruption and difficulties around Thurland Street for almost a year whilst properties were shored up and sewers rerouted for the 'cut and cover' tunnel work necessary there. In November 1895, over £15,000 in compensation was paid out to Messrs Maltby of Thurland Hall Vaults for cellars and their contents damaged during this work.

April 1895 witnessed the start of 13 brick bridges and the 400yd-long Bulwell viaduct

Left:
The MS&L heading for the centre of Nottingham: a view looking north from Sherwood Rise Tunnel towards the site of New Basford station. *NCCLSL*

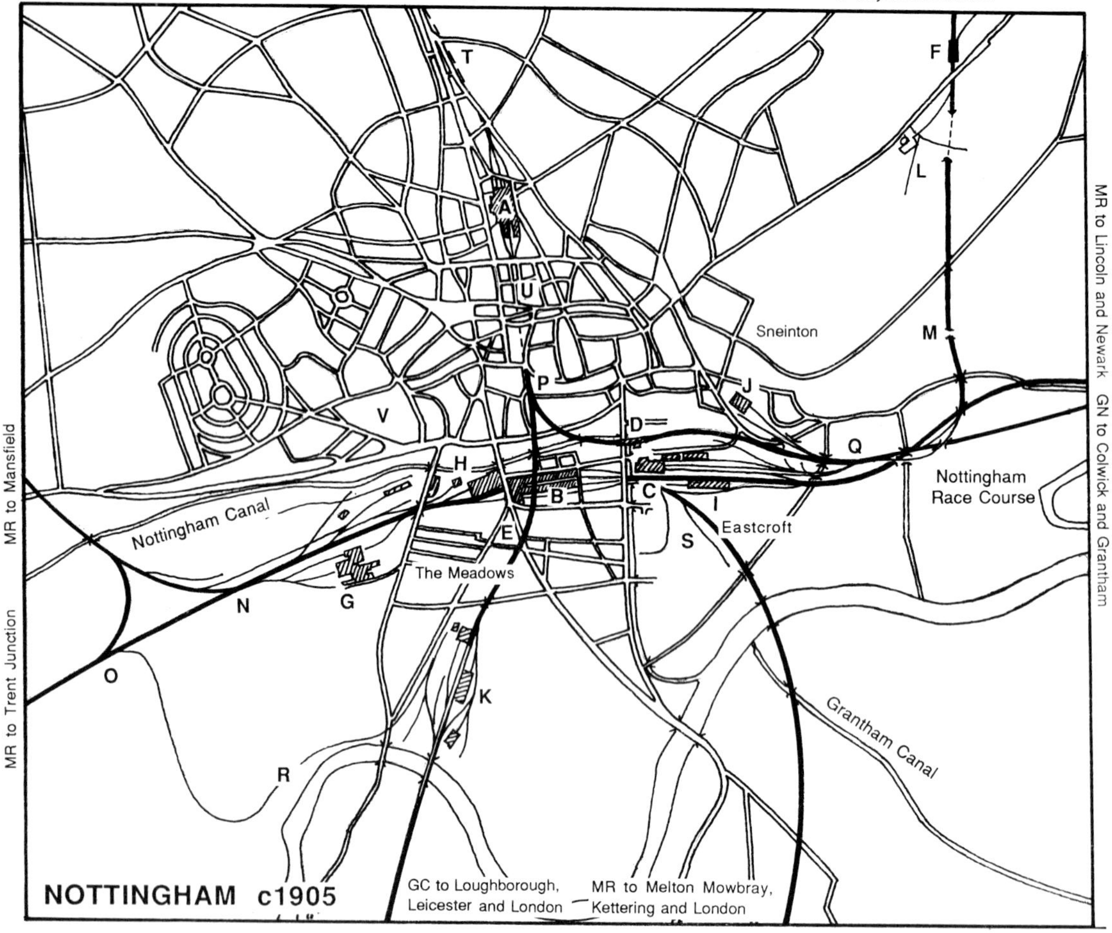

GC to Sheffield

Nottingham Suburban Railway
to Daybrook Junction

MR to Lincoln and Newark GN to Colwick and Grantham

MR to Mansfield

MR to Trent Junction

Sneinton

Nottingham
Race Course

Eastcroft

Nottingham Canal

The Meadows

Grantham Canal

NOTTINGHAM c1905

GC to Loughborough,
Leicester and London

MR to Melton Mowbray,
Kettering and London

A Nottingham Victoria station (GC&GN Joint)
B Nottingham station (MR)
C Nottingham London Road (Low Level)
   station (GN)
D Nottingham London Road (High Level)
   station (GN)
E Arkwright Street station (GC)
F Thorneywood station (Nottingham Suburban
   Railway)
G MR locomotive sheds

H MR goods & grain warehouse & goods yard
I MR carriage sidings & sheds
J LNWR Manvers Street goods yard &
   warehouse
K GC goods yard, warehouse, carriage sheds
   & locomotive sheds
L brickworks
M Sneinton Tunnel (182yd) (Nottingham
   Suburban Railway)
N Mansfield Junction (MR)

O Lenton South Junction (MR)
P Weekday Cross Junction (GC&GN Joint)
Q Trent Lane Junction (GN)
R Clifton Colliery
S Nottingham Corporation Cattle Market &
   Sanitary Department
T Mansfield Road Tunnel (1,189yd) (GC)
U Victoria Street Tunnel (393yd) (GC)
V Nottingham Castle

50

with 25 arches and, by the end of the year, 37 bridges had been completed or were very close to completion. In June 1895 attention turned to the bridging of the River Trent and the MR station and, by October, the foundations for these structures were well advanced. Unfortunately fabrication of the steelwork did not begin until March the following year and erection of the MR bridges did not begin until September. The rest of the line south was almost ready by this time, and it had been intended to use the material excavated from the central station to make up the ground for the new goods yard near the River Trent. As this was not possible, extra land at Ruddington had to be acquired from where the necessary material could be obtained. So that the excavations for Nottingham station would not be delayed either, it was decided to transport spoil northwards to be tipped at Bulwell. This change of plans led to recriminations and, in November 1896, Pollitt (the MS&L's General Manager) made it clear that he held Edward

Parry responsible for not having the steelwork plans for the MR bridges ready in time. Parry, in his turn, blamed the suppliers of the steel — Handyside & Co of Derby — and, at the beginning of 1897, the MS&L minutes record 'serious differences' between Parry and the contractors. Both parties were summoned to London for discussions, and Pollitt decided he would have to make more frequent visits to Nottingham to monitor progress. It wasn't until April 1897 that the first contractors locomotives were able to cross the MR station on the new bridges.

In November 1895, after lengthy negotiations, the GN had finally agreed to take up its option of co-operating with the MS&L to build a joint station in Nottingham. Plans for the station were consequently enlarged and the GN let the contract for building the very awkward connecting line between Trent Lane and Weekday Cross to Nowell & Sons (at a cost of £109,940 5s 3d) in July 1896. As mentioned above, by this time the MS&L viaduct south of Weekday Cross to the

Above right:
A rare view of Linby (GN) station, which was closed to passengers on 1 July 1916, with the GC striding overhead.
LMAG&RS/Newton Collection

Right:
The GC, cutting its way northwards from Thurland Street, passed these buildings on Clinton Street, under Parliament Street in the background, to the site of Nottingham's Central station. *NCCLSL*

MR was complete and the section through the Meadows was proceeding well. This involved 53 brick arches and 12 steelwork spans. Sherwood Rise Tunnel was complete except for its brick portals, the parapet of Bulwell viaduct was being finished off and, in September, when the GN officially approved the plans for the Nottingham Joint station, 50 bridges and 45 culverts were either finished or close to completion.

By Christmas 1896 tunnelling under Nottingham was virtually complete and, in January the following year, Logan & Hemingway applied for a special allowance of £12,561 having had to finish this part of their contract without recourse to the use of explosives. The MS&L agreed to this bonus as they were undoubtedly relieved tunnelling had not caused more problems. Excavation of the site for Nottingham station could then begin and, by working through the night by electric light, the job of removing 580,000cu yd

of spoil was finished in eight months. As elsewhere, the use of steam navvies considerably speeded the work.

On 18 June 1897, at the height of all this work, Nottingham was granted city status to commemorate Queen Victoria's Diamond Jubilee. Then on 1 August the MS&L changed its name becoming the Great Central Railway and, flushed with the success of its rapid station excavations, Logan & Hemingway applied for another bonus. The GC agreed, but its joint partners the GN were reluctant to contribute. Offended at this, the GC argued that the contractor was entitled to claim from the GN as it was the latter who had delayed the work of planning and excavation by becoming involved in the station project so late. The GN remained unmoved and, of the £20,000 eventually paid to the contractor, £12,500 came from the GC and £7,500 from the Nottingham Joint Station Committee.

Left:
The site of Victoria station looking northeast in 1897, with Union Road carried across the excavations on a temporary bridge. The GC hotel will later occupy the area in the foreground.
NCCLSL/14026

Above right:
The GC's twin double-track bridges across the River Trent pictured with a line of contractors' wagons in the spring of 1897.
LMAG&RS/Newton Collection

Right:
Looking east from beneath Carrington Street bridge early in 1897 at the GC's new bridge across the MR's 1848 station.
LMAG&RS/Newton Collection

Below:
The site of Carrington station, in the autumn of 1896, looking due north from the top of Mansfield Road tunnel towards Sherwood Rise tunnel.
LMAG&RS/Newton Collection

stone dressings, whilst the materials of the interior, glazed bricks, buff-coloured terracotta, and faience had been supplied by Burmantofts of Leeds (one of the country's most renowned firms producing this sort of material). The steel for the overall roofs — made up of two 63ft wide spans and one central 84ft wide span 40ft above platform level, and the decorative end screens — had been fabricated by the Horseley Co Ltd of Tipton, and glazed by Mellowes & Co of Sheffield. The individual awnings over the platforms were supplied and fitted by Handyside & Co of Derby.

The large booking hall had seven ticket issuing windows, three for each company and one for excursions. A wide lattice footbridge connected this hall to the two island platforms below, each with double track bays at either end. On the platforms were refreshment rooms, dining and tea rooms with attached kitchens, waiting rooms, lavatories, and numerous offices, and beneath the platforms, connected to them by hydraulic lifts, ran a tunnel for the transfer of luggage and parcels to and from the main buildings on Milton Street. Every last detail had been carefully worked out to combine efficiency of operation with aesthetic harmony; the two signalboxes in the centre of the station ('West' on the down platform, 'East' on the up platform) looked from the outside like bay windows, and even the north and south signalboxes although containing standard equipment were not built to the company's standard design, displaying their own architectural pretensions with deep overhanging eaves.

In financial terms the price of this lavish station is known to have exceeded one million pounds but the environmental cost of the site and the route of the GC through Nottingham had been the demolition of 1,300 mainly slum houses, St Stephen's church and schools, the 1840 Union Workhouse, the Guildhall, the ragged school, at least 24 public houses, and six years of disruption. It was a fact that 125 new houses were erected around Woodborough Road and 175 in the Meadows area by Arnold & Son of Doncaster, but as *The Nottingham Daily Guardian* recorded at the opening of Victoria station: '...scarcely one of these houses has been occupied by the people who were dispossessed of their old dwellings, the rents of the new cottages being at least double those of the old.'

Finally, by the spring of 1898, work was sufficiently advanced for tenders to be invited for the prestigious job of constructing Nottingham station. In March the tender of £146,918 submitted by Henry Lovatt, who was just completing contract No 2 for the line between East Leake and Aylestone, was accepted. By then most of the bridges across the station site were well advanced, including Parliament Street, and Lovatt was able to start his work almost immediately. On 26 July 1898 the first coal train ran over the new line between Annesley and London and, when it opened to passengers on 15 March 1899, Arkwright Street and Carrington had to serve as Nottingham's first GC stations for over a year before the central station was complete. Work on this continued on apace despite a number of strikes and many days lost because of bad weather and, eventually, on 24 May 1900, the Queen's birthday, with the booking office and clock tower still incomplete Nottingham's central railway station was opened. At the altogether sensible suggestion of the Town Clerk it was christened Victoria.

To Edward Parry and Nottingham Corporation, Victoria station was the *central* station they had been pressing for since 1881. The MS&L minutes had always referred to the central station in Nottingham long before the company changed its name to Great Central Railway. Central described the site, and it was just a coincidence that this working title also reflected the new name of the MS&L after 1897.

Along with the rest of the railway, Victoria station was superbly engineered and constructed, and worthy of any progressive city at the turn of the century. The exterior was built of Nottingham red pressed bricks and Darley Dale

Left:
Goose Fair crowds in October 1898 at the GN's London Road terminus just five months before passenger trains were diverted into Nottingham Victoria station.
LMAG&RS/Newton Collection

Below left:
A rare view, taken in 1921, of London Road station in use as the GN's goods depot. *Ian Allan Library*

Bottom:
The GN's London Road (High Level) station on 1 September 1955, seen with a sign encouraging passengers to 'Alight here for Trent Bridge cricket and football grounds'.
R. M. Casserley

Left:
Nottingham Victoria Joint station almost complete and ready for its opening on 24 May 1900. *LPC/Ian Allan Library*

Below left:
A photograph which captures fully Victoria station's impressive internal space. *Real Photos/Ian Allan Library*

Bottom:
Assembled in May 1900 at the GC's Gorton Works, this American Baldwin 2-6-0 No 956 was, like Nottingham Victoria station, only a few weeks old when photographed. *Bucknall Collection/Ian Allan Library*

Left:
**Nottingham Victoria
station, c1904.**
NCCLSL/35944

Bottom:
**The signals controlled from
Nottingham Victoria West
signalbox were still intact
when this photograph was
taken a few months before
the station closed.**
D. J. Powell

Left:
The West signalbox on platform No 4, Nottingham Victoria, from a photograph which appeared in Burmantoft's 1902 catalogue. *Ironbridge Gorge Museum Trust*

If lavish described Nottingham Victoria, then optimistic described the GC's arrangements for goods, rolling stock and locomotives. Twin bridges carried independent double track passenger and goods lines over the Trent just east of Wilford Road bridge. Immediately north of the river a 33-acre site adjacent to Queen's Walk was laid out for goods, carriage and engine facilities. At the north end of the site where the goods and passenger lines joined, an impressive three-storey warehouse was constructed, and at the south end one of the country's first electrically-driven travelling cranes was installed with a capacity of 25 tons. On the opposite side of the lines a seven-road carriage shed was erected and, just below this, within whistling distance of the MR engine sheds, the GC provided accommodation for 16 of its own locomotives.

Living in a generation which has witnessed the complete loss of Nottingham Victoria and the GC main line through the city because it was thought an unnecessary duplication, it is all too easy to forget that when the station and goods yard were planned, passenger traffic by rail was growing, the electric tram had not yet creamed off the commuter trade, most of industry's raw materials and finished products travelled by rail, and no one could have anticipated a four-year world war that would so fundamentally change society.

Victoria station was designed to handle the 170 passenger trains a day coming in from both the GN and GC and comfortably fulfil the role of a true interchange station. In fact, considerable effort had been expended getting GN trains into Victoria. North of Nottingham connections

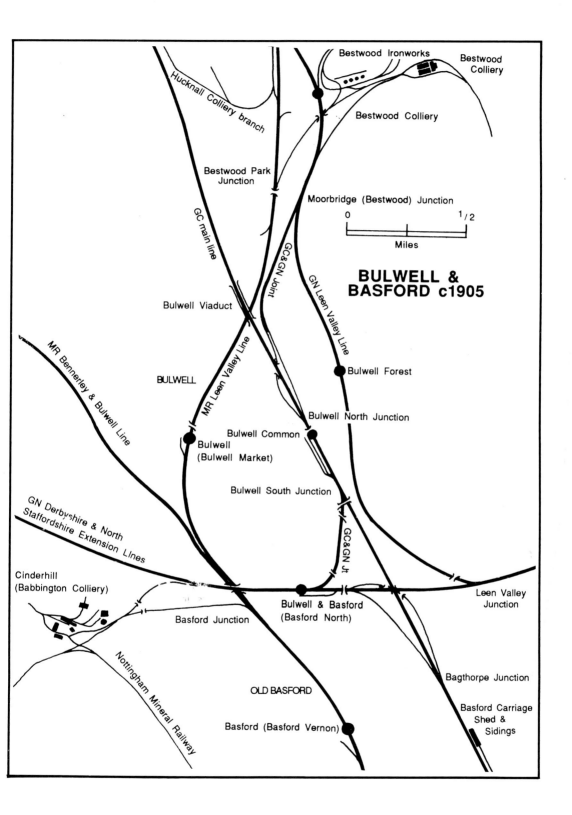

BULWELL & BASFORD c1905

Bestwood Ironworks

Bestwood Colliery

Bestwood Colliery

Hucknall Colliery branch

Bestwood Park Junction

Moorbridge (Bestwood) Junction

0   1/2

Miles

GC main line

GC&GN Joint

GN Leen Valley Line

Bulwell Viaduct

MR Bennerley & Bulwell Line

BULWELL

MR Leen Valley Line

Bulwell Forest

Bulwell North Junction

Bulwell Common

Bulwell (Bulwell Market)

Bulwell South Junction

GN Derbyshire & North Staffordshire Extension Lines

GC&GN Jt

Cinderhill (Babbington Colliery)

Basford Junction

Bulwell & Basford (Basford North)

Leen Valley Junction

Nottingham Mineral Railway

OLD BASFORD

Bagthorpe Junction

Basford (Basford Vernon)

Basford Carriage Shed & Sidings

59

Left:
The interior of one of the dining rooms at Nottingham Victoria as shown in Burmantoft's 1902 catalogue. *Ironbridge Gorge Museum Trust*

Below left:
Atlantic No 1086, photographed at Nottingham Victoria in c1923.
T. G. Hepburn/Rail Archive Stephenson

Bottom:
If there were GN four-wheeled carriages behind the tender, then the train must have been destined for Skegness, Sutton-on-Sea and/or Mablethorpe! Here GN 'D2' 4-4-0 No 1316 approaches Radcliffe-on-Trent in 1922 bound for the East Coast. *Real Photos/Ian Allan Library*

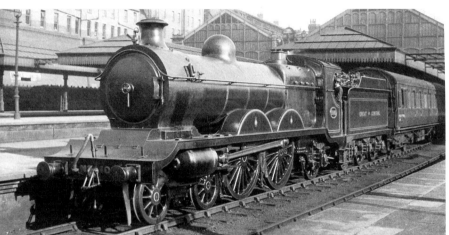

between the two companies were formed at Bulwell, where separate up and down lines left the GC at Bagthorpe Junction joining the GN at Basford & Bulwell station, (Bulwell North), the up spur earning the nickname 'rathole' as it burrowed through a short tunnel under the GC. Another spur (jointly owned) ran north from Basford & Bulwell joining the GC at Bulwell South Junction and, just north of there, another split junction (jointly owned) connected with the GN's Leen Valley line at Moorbridge Junction, Bestwood. To the south of Victoria at Weekday Cross, another spur left the GC to run across the Nottingham Canal, through London Road High Level station adjacent to the original AN&B&EJR terminus, behind the Corporation gas works on a steel viaduct which straddled the sidings to these works, to join the GN at Trent Lane Junction. As well as diverting all its local traffic from the 'Ambergate' terminus, (renamed London Road [Low Level]), the GN used this connection with the GC from 15 March 1899 for four southbound and two northbound expresses between King's Cross and Manchester. When Victoria station opened, the 11.4am ex-Nottingham ran non-stop to London in 2hr 26min.

In comparison the first GC expresses had to run to comparatively slow schedules as the new main line consolidated and, therefore, the fastest time between Nottingham and London, Marylebone, was a lengthy 3hr 6min. Nevertheless, by the time Victoria was operational, this schedule had been cut to 2hr 39min. Between Nottingham and Manchester the journey was reduced to 1hr 59min but, realising it could better this, the MR diverted some of its London-Manchester trains away from Leicester and through Nottingham providing a 1hr 45min service between there and Manchester. The MR's Bradford and Sheffield trains which, since 1880, had traditionally taken the Melton Mowbray line, suffered badly from GC competition. Nottingham-Bradford by GC took 2hr 11min compared with the fastest MR train which took 2hr 30min, and Nottingham-Sheffield occupied just 52min by GC and exactly one hour by MR. A journey by GC between Nottingham and Leicester was also considerably faster than by the MR.

Nottingham also benefited from a number of cross-country services established by the GC when its new link with the GWR at Banbury opened in 1901. These included a York-Southampton service, from 1902 a Newcastle-Bournemouth express and, in 1905, a service between Newcastle and Cardiff. In 1907 the GC even began a through service from Marylebone to Lincoln by slipping a carriage off the 3.20pm at Leicester, working it forward to Victoria and attaching it there to the 6pm Nottingham-Lincoln train via Duckmanton Junction and the LD&ECR (absorbed by the GC that year). By this route Lincoln was 4hr 36min from the capital, hardly any competition for the GN's three-hour schedule via Grantham.

The MR response

Whilst the MS&L London Extension was under construction, the MR had three significant local projects in hand. These were the erection of a new passenger station at Hucknall, a new goods warehouse next to Carrington Street bridge and another locomotive shed next to Wilford Road, Nottingham. There were no plans for a new passenger station for the city.

By the end of the 19th century Hucknall Torkard had established itself as the most important town in the Leen Valley coalfield. Between 1871 and 1881 its population had more than doubled and, in the next decade, it rose again by 3,000, to stand at 13,094 in 1891. This trend, combined with rising passenger receipts and the approach of the MS&L, encouraged the MR to secure an Act in 1893 to renew its station there. Work began the following summer and, anticipating the design of the MS&L's London Extension country stations, the up and down lines were laid either side of a wide single platform accessed from a new road bridge over the line. The station buildings on this platform were provided with substantial iron and glass canopies. A new goods shed and stationmaster's house were built at the same time and, when the station opened on 29 December 1895, it had cost the MR just over £15,000.

At the same time, J. Dickenson of Derby was fully occupied erecting the MR's impressive new goods and grain warehouse adjacent to Carrington Street bridge. This was part of a major remodelling of the goods facilities at Nottingham approved by the MR in 1893; Dickenson's tender of £42,815 13s was accepted on 15 March 1894. The combined floor area of the two-storey building had been calculated at 1⅓ acres (or 6,333sq yd), the first floor being supported on only 39 cast-iron columns. Stylistically, the building closely followed contemporary MR practice with red brick walls, cast-iron windows and slate roofs (four in this case). At the east end of the building a number of traversers were installed to replace the use of wagon turntables, and the building was equipped with the latest hydraulic cranes and electric lighting. Separating the existing goods office fronting Carrington Street and the new warehouse, a low building was constructed with a number of shallow ridge and furrow roofs. All was brought into use on 13 April 1896, followed a little later by the reorganisation

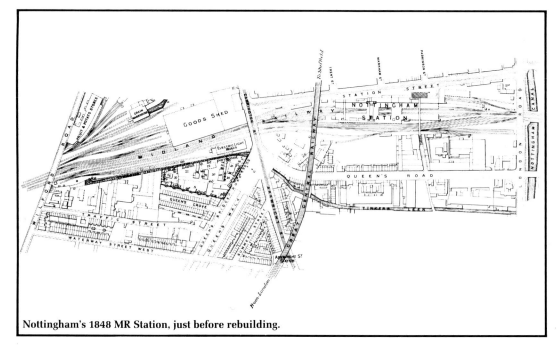

Nottingham's 1848 MR Station, just before rebuilding.

of the coal depot (Goods Yard West) and the cattle docks (Goods Yard East). Dickenson also received the contract to extend the Bonded Store which was presumably also finished at about this time.

At its locomotive department, a third engine shed for 24 locomotives was provided in 1893, after the MR had reconsidered its 1891 plan to build a shed for 48 engines and, at the end of 1900, it was agreed to purchase extra land at Beeston for an engine shed and more sidings there.

But, impressive though the new goods station was, and, however necessary the new locomotive shed, with the arrival of the GC in Nottingham, the erection of Victoria station and the fast services offered by the new company, the MR was obviously embarrassed by the comparison between its passenger services and station facilities. It had known for some time that many of its main line stations were outdated and inadequate to deal with increasing traffic and would need rebuilding but, perhaps, it regretted starting with Leicester station first in 1892-95 when Nottingham Victoria turned out to be far larger than its counterpart in Leicester and did so completely overshadow the MR's 1848 Nottingham station.

Having said this, in 1897 when the plans of Victoria station were known, the MR was only asking for Parliamentary approval for extra goods lines through its Nottingham station and, in January the following year, when the com-

pany laid plans before the City Corporation for a new road from the corner of Broad Marsh and Carrington Street in a straight line to its station buildings on Station Street, it all seemed to indicate that the company had no immediate plans for new premises on Carrington Street bridge. The new road was not built and the MR resisted fundamental change for another three years until, in April 1902, the Way & Works Committee recorded the General Purposes Committee's approval for an expenditure of £198,000 on reconstructing Nottingham station.

On 24 July 1902 the contract for widening Carrington Street bridge was let to the Butterley Co for £4,550 15s, followed on 23 January 1903 by the first of six contracts for the new station buildings, awarded to Edward Wood & Sons of Park Street, Derby, (at £44,357 15s 1d) — a contractor who had long enjoyed MR patronage for work in and around Nottingham. The 65-page contract document gave detailed specifications for the entrance buildings on Carrington Street:

'All terracotta and glazed brick work generally must be walled with as close joints as possible and no joint, whether vertical or horizontal, is to exceed ⅛th of an inch in thickness and shall be pointed with Keene's cement or putty coloured to match the shade of the adjoining facework.

'All masonry facework of Derbyshire Grit from Old Darley Dale Quarries. Load

Above:
A view looking west to the new Carrington Street road bridge, probably at the beginning of 1903, as work begins on the MR's new station. The signalbox is of particular interest. *NCCLSL/2112*

Right:
At Radcliffe-on-Trent, Stationmaster Mr Salmon (centre) poses awkwardly with other members of his GN staff next to a LNWR notice board in c1910. *NCCLSL*

Below right:
The GC's Bulwell Common station. *NCCLSL/80807*

Left:
One of the MR's handsome 'Spinner' 4-2-2s No 178, its tender stacked high with coal, is ready for a 123.5 mile dash to St Pancras in September 1906.
F. H. Gillford/John Marshall Collection

bearing masonry, eg girder beds, gritstone from Whatstandwell, Matlock.

'All deals and battens for floorboards and scantlings shall be the best carefully selected 'Redwood'. The Oak used is to be best Austrian Wainscot. The Walnut to be best American. Mahogany to be Cuba, and is to include French polishing. The Teak to be Indian, and is to include twice oiling.

'The whole of the steel shall be of a mild and tough quality, made from the best description of British iron only...'

Kirk, Knight & Co of Sleaford received the contract for construction of the buildings on platforms Nos 4 and 5 on 18 June 1903, (£14,319 12s 10d) and the final contract dated 16 September 1903 for the erection of buildings on platforms Nos 1 and 3 (£11,563 12s) was awarded to Wood & Sons. Construction then advanced extremely rapidly. The parcels office on Station Street, erected by Kirk, Knight & Co, opened in November, and the rest of the station was ready for an official opening on 17 January 1904, just under a year since the first contract had been let.

The architect of both Nottingham Victoria and the new MR station was A. E. Lambert and, not surprisingly, the two buildings shared many details in common, the most noticeable being the style of elliptical arches on the façades and the window and door openings on the platform buildings which were enlivened by projecting segments and keystones.

The layout of the MR station followed the formula first seen at Leicester, with an impressive red terracotta façade surmounted by a clock tower (fronting Carrington Street) on a wide new bridge over the railway. Six arched openings — the two beneath the tower with pairs of rusti-

cated columns echoing those on each corner of the tower — gave access to the covered cab approach, or '*porte-cochère*', and the booking hall. The latter was an area 104½ft x 42ft finished with buff coloured walls, dark green glazed tiles (or faience) and dark brown skirting, with eight ticket windows — five for various third-class destinations, one for first-class, one for excursions and one left in reserve. (The station remained an 'open' one until 1917.) Like Victoria station there were two wide island platforms but, in this case, there was only one single track bay platform at the east end of the station and an extra platform on the southside. All but this platform (No 6) and the bay were covered by separate awnings fabricated by Handyside & Co of Derby. Two footbridges (by the Phoenix Co of Derby) connected all platforms, the most easterly one with its own ticket office also acting as the public thoroughfare between Queen's Road and Station Street and, just to the east of this, connected directly to the parcels office, was an independent luggage and parcels bridge with hydraulic lifts. All the rooms in the platform buildings for waiting, refreshment facilities and lavatories were lavishly furnished and equipped in solid and stolid Edwardian taste. As at Victoria station and the MR's Leicester station, there were two signalboxes midway along the island platforms, in this case 'A' and 'B'.

Like Victoria, the new MR station was designed to handle comfortably large numbers of passengers patronising 162 inward and outward trains every working weekday, augmented by specials during the holiday season. As well as the local services, the MR made much of its three London expresses complete with either breakfast, luncheon or dining cars attached, departing at 8.25am, 1.10pm and 8.10pm, and reaching St Pancras via Melton Mowbray in 2hr

20min. This compared favourably with the GN's fastest service which left Nottingham Victoria at 11.4am and reached King's Cross in 2hr 26min, but both companies' trains were overshadowed by the GC's 2hr 14min service between Marylebone and Nottingham running at an average speed of 56mph. Rather than dampen the competitive spirit, however, the MR continued to clip minutes off its express schedules between Nottingham and London via Melton Mowbray until, by 1914, it could boast an express covering the 123.5 miles in just 2hr 12min.

Without a doubt this was the fastest prewar service of the three major companies operating between Nottingham and the capital but, if neither the GN, GC nor MR gave satisfaction, there was another more leisurely London service operated by the LNWR. Leaving London Road (Low Level) station at 9am and running over the GN&LNWR a traveller could arrive at Euston 3hr

45min later at 12.45pm without having to change trains, and return at 4.30pm to arrive back in Nottingham at 8.16pm. Competition for competition's sake, or did people actually use these through carriages?

Friendly rivalry must have also extended to the railway staff and, between June 1903 and the spring of 1904, an optimistic publication, called *The Nottingham & District Railway Journal*, provided '...a medium of intercourse between the various sections of railway workers in the service of the four lines running into Nottingham...'. Paragraphs entitled 'Central Scribblings', 'Midland Musings', and 'Northern Notes' profiled the careers of various staff and recorded the tussles of the obviously popular company cricket clubs. For example, on 6 June 1903, the GC beat the GN by nine runs, a tight contest considering the GC only scored 45, and on 18 July the GN Clerks team took their revenge on the MR locomen's team by beating them 64 to 55 runs!

These were good years for all the railway companies in Nottingham. In 1899 a record 1,157,775 passengers were booked at the MR's station creating a revenue of £119,375 against station expenses of only £16,955, the Goods Department making £181,541, its highest amount that century, against expenditure of £53,682. These impressive statistics were not repeated again until World War 1 but, although increased expenditure at the new Nottingham station did reduce profits, passenger numbers still averaged well over one million per annum. Comparative figures do not survive for the GN and GC, unfortunately, but there is every reason to believe they fared just as well during this period, and the LNWR no doubt made something out of its Northampton trains.

Freight traffic

On the freight side, private sidings continued to be very important revenue earners for all the companies serving Nottingham and a number of important additions were made in this period. For example, in 1896 the Raleigh Cycle Co moved to its new factory next to the MR's Leen Valley line at Radford, whilst Taylor Brothers Ltd established its Midland Foundry next to the railway at Sandiacre to produce all types of metal fabrications including railway permanent way, and the following year the Beeston Boiler Co Ltd, established in 1888, moved to new premises served by sidings off the MR, its products selling to both the home and export market. By 1904 when the first edition of *The Railway Clearing House Handbook of Railway Stations*

appeared, 41 private sidings, in addition to railway company stations and sidings, were listed under the Nottingham heading. The City Corporation was particularly well served with sidings off the MR into its Health Department and into the large gas works at Basford, into the Sanitary Department in Eastcroft, and off the GN into the hospital site at Daybrook and into the sewage works near Netherfield and Colwick.

Beer, bicycles, fish, fruit, cigarettes, cattle, milk and all manner of machines travelled through and originated from the city, but coal continued to dominate the Nottingham railway scene. At the end of the century the MR particularly invested heavily in the modernisation of its facilities transforming many of its operating practices at the same time. In 1899 there were 70 shunting horses at Toton but, in 1901, the yard was converted for 'hump' working. About the same time plans had been drawn up for another two roundhouses there but, in the event, only one was built and equipped with a 55ft turntable. Then, in the next few years, the MR finally managed to stitch together its various sections of goods lines to provide completely independent double lines for passenger and goods traffic along most of the Erewash Valley, including the connecting of the goods lines south of Trent with Toton yard, a task allocated on 20 April 1899 to Henry Lovatt for £49,161 1s 3d, and completed by early 1902. This was followed by the introduction of the MR's famous Train Control System which considerably increased the efficient running of freight and especially coal trains on these new lines.

The GN also continued to handle huge quantities of mineral traffic and, at the end of 1896, Dennett & Ingle was awarded the contract to

Right:
Part of the MR's extensive goods facilities in Nottingham photographed from Wilford Road bridge on 27 March 1922. Apart from the through lines in the foreground, the site will — in the mid-1990s — be occupied by the city's new Magistrates' Courts and Bridewell. *Crown Copyright, courtesy National Railway Museum/DY12458*

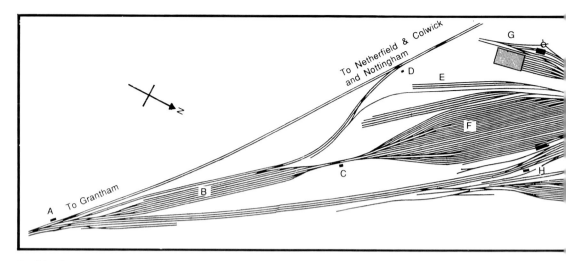

build a large new engine shed, wagon shops and associated buildings at Colwick for £15,481. At the turn of the century the first colliery east of Nottingham, at Gedling next to the GN's Derbyshire Extension line, began to produce coal, and Colwick yard was enlarged again. Twenty-nine extra sidings were laid out for the accommodation of another 1,000 wagons, bringing the total capacity of the yard to over 6,000 wagons. The increase in coal traffic combined with passenger trains meant the double line between Colwick and Leen Valley Junction became very congested. To increase line capacity the GN opened a new signalbox called Mapperley, 100yd east of the tunnel, on 31 October 1899 to break an already short block section and control just the down line used by empty coal trains returning to the collieries of both the Erewash and Leen valleys. This still proved insufficient and, on 8 September 1907, the GN introduced tandem coal train working, whereby two empty coal trains could be coupled together at Colwick Yard, Locomotive Junction, Colwick North, Arno Vale or Leen Valley Junction signalboxes for Leen Valley Junction, Bulwell Forest, Awsworth Junction and/or Digby signalboxes. The special GN circular authorising this made it clear that two trains going in the same direction had to be coupled together, and that it was the responsibility of the guard of the first train to couple the engine of the second train to his brakevan. The skill of the two engine crews must have been taxed to the limits, but what a sight two trains so coupled must have made pulling out of Colwick yard and storming up the gradient to Mapperley tunnel.

Colwick yard was probably never busier and, during World War 1, there were 400 staff employed in shunting and marshalling operations in addition to over 1,000 men in the loco-

motive department. Close to 260 engines were shedded there, mostly 0-6-0s (seven of which acted as pilots), 2-6-0s, 4-4-0s for passenger work, and a number of Ivatt's large 0-8-2Ts. It was estimated that over 40 up and nearly 70 down trains regularly left Colwick every day for Peterborough, Doncaster, Boston, Lincoln, Whitemoor, Ferme Park and other local destinations, and on a single busy day in November 1913, no less than 209 trains were dealt with. In addition to coal, huge quantities of iron ore passed through to Stanton, (the company making 100,000 tons of cast-iron pipes in 1905) as well as large consignments of vegetables from the eastern counties dispatched to Derby, Sheffield and Manchester.

Competition and World War 1

In 1896 Nottingham Corporation had deposited a bill to acquire the town's tramways and, on 18 October 1897, they were formally handed over to the new city. By May the following year plans had been unveiled to double various sections and extend the system, and by 1900 work was in hand to substitute horse traction with electric tramcars. This work, especially the laying of new tracks, caused considerable inconvenience along some of the city's busiest roads, and it must have seemed all the more tiresome following on from, as it did, the disruption started by the MS&L back in 1894.

Nevertheless, the new electric tram service proved very popular, and patronage of railway stations within the city boundaries suffered accordingly. The MR stations at Radford, Lenton, Bulwell and Basford were badly affected, the latter also having to contend with the opening of GC stations close by. In 1895, 50,322, 29,094, 125,455 and 111,156 passengers

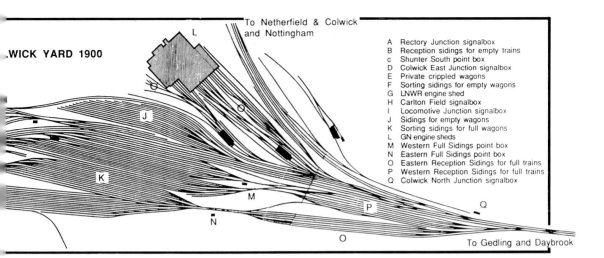

To Netherfield & Colwick and Nottingham

A Rectory Junction signalbox
B Reception sidings for empty trains
c Shunter South point box
D Colwick East Junction signalbox
E Private crippled wagons
F Sorting sidings for empty wagons
G LNWR engine shed
H Carlton Field signalbox
I Locomotive Junction signalbox
J Sidings for empty wagons
K Sorting sidings for full wagons
L GN engine sheds
M Western Full Sidings point box
N Eastern Full Sidings point box
O Eastern Reception Sidings for full trains
P Western Reception Sidings for full trains
Q Colwick North Junction signalbox

To Gedling and Daybrook

Wilford Road bridge looking south from the end of the 'fruit & potato stores' platform. Behind the wagons is the stockade which separated the through lines from the goods yard (see previous photograph), and behind that Wilford Road signalbox. *Nottingham Evening Post*

were booked at these stations respectively; by 1907 the figures had dropped to 21,216, 14,207, 80,474 and 71,449 respectively. This downward trend persisted as travellers continued to desert the trains for trams. Radford and Bulwell's worst returns of 11,630 and 73,611 were recorded in 1912 before both stations recovered strongly during and after World War 1. In the case of Basford, passenger numbers continued to decline throughout the period, falling by more than 50% between 1908 and 1918 (from 65,561 to 30,602) before showing any signs of steadying. But this was nothing compared with the losses at Lenton. From 14,207 in 1907, the number of passengers booked dropped by half to 7,160 in just a year, and in 1910 only 2,446 people patronised the station. The much reduced staff soldiered on until the end of June 1911 when the MR finally admitted defeat, and the first station within the city boundaries closed to passenger traffic. Although figures are not available, similar reductions in passenger numbers must have affected the GC's Bulwell Common, New Basford and Carrington stations as well as the GN's Daybrook and Basford & Bulwell stations, although it was the country station at Linby which the GN closed to passengers on 1 July 1916.

Patronage of the Nottingham Suburban Railway also suffered, initially from the coming of the GC and then from Corporation tram competition. Once the former had opened, the Suburban line lost its usefulness as a through route. Then, at the end of 1910, trams reached Thorneywood station and, in January 1915, Daybrook and Arnold could be reached by tram from outside Nottingham Victoria. It probably came as no surprise and caused no hardship, when, as a wartime economy measure, Thorneywood, St Ann's Well and Sherwood stations were closed to passengers on 13 July 1916. J. A. B. Hamilton writing about the railways of Nottingham in the March 1932 edition of *The Railway Magazine* recalled that when he wanted to buy a ticket from Nottingham Victoria to Sherwood, just before the passenger service was withdrawn, the booking clerk advised him to go by tram!

In complete contrast, however, it is interesting to note the increasing number of passengers using stations at places unaffected by trams. For example, in 1896 1,286 season tickets were sold at Beeston, 268,070 passengers were booked and £10,870 was made in ticket sales. By 1907 1,751 season tickets were in use, 408,917 passengers had bought tickets and revenue from these sales had risen to £16,044. The same was true at Long Eaton station where the number of passengers booked almost doubled between 1896 and 1907, and there was a similar upward trend at Stanton Gate and Stapleford & Sandiacre. Even at Trent ticket sales increased by almost 50% in the same period, rising from 165,306 to 336,226. In these outlying districts it was not until after World War 1 with the arrival of the motorbuses that passenger numbers began to tail off significantly.

On 1 January 1917 the passenger service over the MR's Basford-Bennerley Junction route was withdrawn and the tracks west of Kimberley sta-

Left:
A welcome break in activity at the MR's Wilford Road goods yard on 31 March 1922. Nothing of this yard remains in railway use today. *Crown Copyright, courtesy National Railway Museum/DY12476*

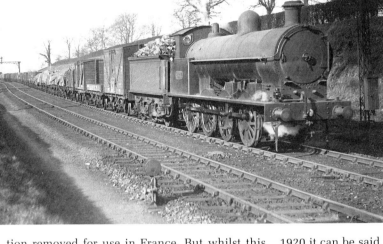

tion removed for use in France. But whilst this was happening another MR station found that it could hardly cope with an upturn in its business. As tracks were being taken up near Kimberley, new ones were being laid at Chilwell to serve the National Shell Filling Factory. The factory was fully operational by October 1916 employing 6,000 people of whom 2,000 were women, this figure rising to 10,000 including 4,000 women by 1918, many getting to and from work by the numerous special trains between the city, Ilkeston and Derby. The little country station at Attenborough, which had dealt with just over 30,000 passengers in 1915, found itself coming to terms with over 84,000 the following year and photographs show just how crowded the station platforms became even after they were extended. As passenger numbers increased so too did the number of ammunition trains dealing with Chilwell's estimated annual output of over a million tons. But all this activity inside and outside the works was at some considerable risk, as was tragically demonstrated on 1 July 1918 when 134 people were killed and 250 injured in a massive explosion in the factory.

Summing up the period between 1894 and 1920 it can be said that in just a few years either side of the turn of the century, Nottingham had gained a new fast and reliable main line, two fine large modern stations and had within the city boundaries 17 stations all benefiting from a generous passenger service. Without a doubt the Edwardian era saw Nottingham's railways at their zenith; but the halcyon days were short-lived. When the City Corporation undertook a survey of the number of passengers travelling from local railway stations into Nottingham between 7am and 9.30am on two consecutive days in January 1920, they discovered that approximately 130 travelled in from the MR's Carlton station, just over 1,000 from the GN's Netherfield station nearby, but an astonishing 5,250 used the Carlton Road tram route into the city between 5.30am and 9am. Just over 3,900 used the trams from Arnold compared with under 200 from the GN's Daybrook station. With the introduction of the motor- and trolleybus, and for those who could afford it the private car, the number of people travelling by train continued to fall throughout the interwar period undermining the viability of local railway services and leading to significant rationalisation.

8. 1921-45 The Grouping Era

The interwar period was a difficult time for the country's railways. World War 1 had profoundly changed many prewar attitudes and the British society which emerged after the conflict was very different from the one which had so confidently thrust a new main line through the heart of Nottingham only 20 years before. The railways hardly had time to recover from state control and the introduction of the eight-hour working day before the Grouping of 1923 created its own administrative upheavals. Then followed the General Strike of 1926, the financial crash of 1929 and the demoralising Depression of the 1930s when adequate investment in modernisation was hardly possible. LMS passenger receipts fell to their lowest interwar level in 1932, followed by freight in 1933. It is not surprising, therefore, that outwardly the railways of Nottingham appeared to continue as before with the GN and GC uniting readily as the LNER and the MR apparently going about its normal business but with a different name. Operationally the Grouping seemed almost academic as the four ex-LNWR trains each way between Northampton/Market Harborough and Nottingham operated by the LMS continued to run into the LNER's London Road (Low Level) station, and the ex-M&GN Yarmouth-Nottingham trains, operated by the LNER after 1936, continued to steam into the LMS station.

But this continuity was really a form of inflexibility, indicating a certain lack of vision in contrast to that which characterised the road hauliers and City Corporation. Combined with lack of investment it meant that the railway companies serving Nottingham never really met the challenges of a changing society. For example, despite having numerous branch lines around the city, neither the LMS nor the LNER made any attempt to emulate the GWR in its successful use of diesel railcars during the 1930s. When the LNER did experiment with railcars it stuck doggedly to steam power, using railcars supplied by the Clayton Wagon Co and Sentinel, which, when compared with the GWR streamlined units and to contemporary double-deck buses, looked very dated. And when the LMS finally introduced its diesel multiple-unit in startling aluminium and Post Office red livery just before World War 2, it was obviously not designed to potter about on branch lines, making six fast runs from St Pancras daily including the 2.45pm Leicester-Nottingham service returning as the 5.25pm Nottingham-London. Whilst the private motorbus operators and Nottingham City Council took the lead in urban transport progressing from trams to trolleybuses and motorbuses in just a few years, the LNER continued to rattle its passengers around the fringes of the city in ex-GN carriages until almost the outbreak of the War.

Right:
Corporation services, like this one along Colwick Road (photographed sometime between 1933 and June 1935 with the ex-MR's Lincoln line in the background), led to many commuters deserting the railways for trams before World War 1. *P. Collins Collection*

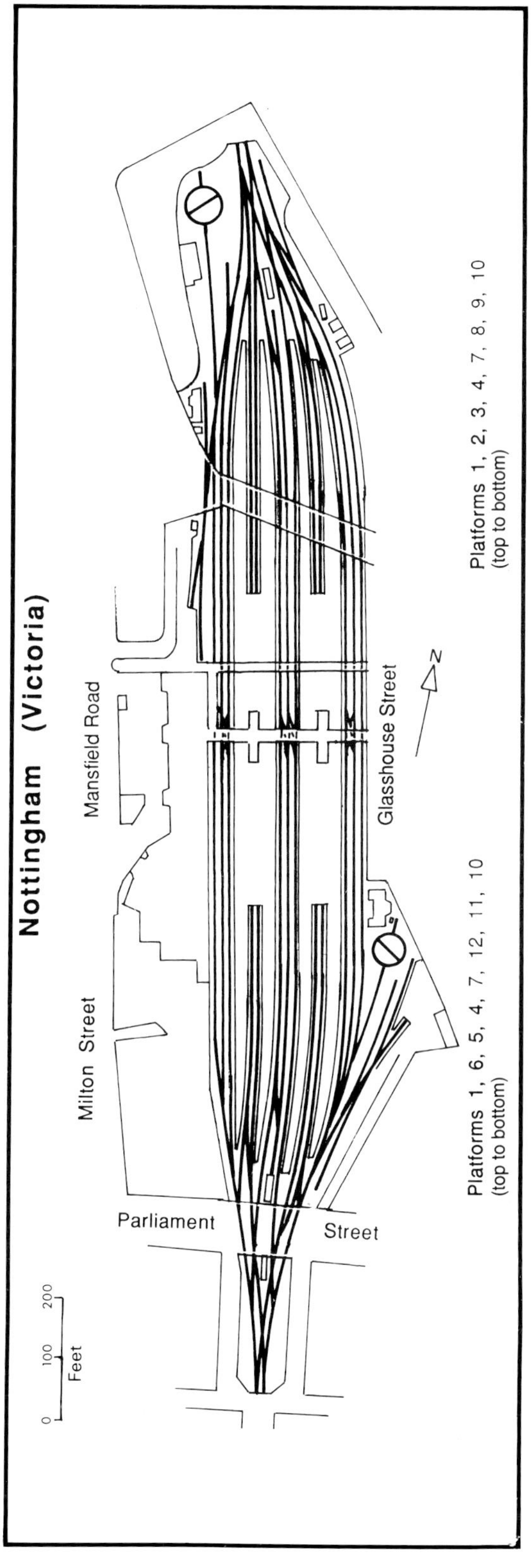
Nottingham (Victoria)
Mansfield Road
Milton Street
Glasshouse Street
N
Platforms 1, 2, 3, 4, 7, 8, 9, 10
(top to bottom)
Platforms 1, 6, 5, 4, 7, 12, 11, 10
(top to bottom)
Parliament
Street
0
100
200
Feet

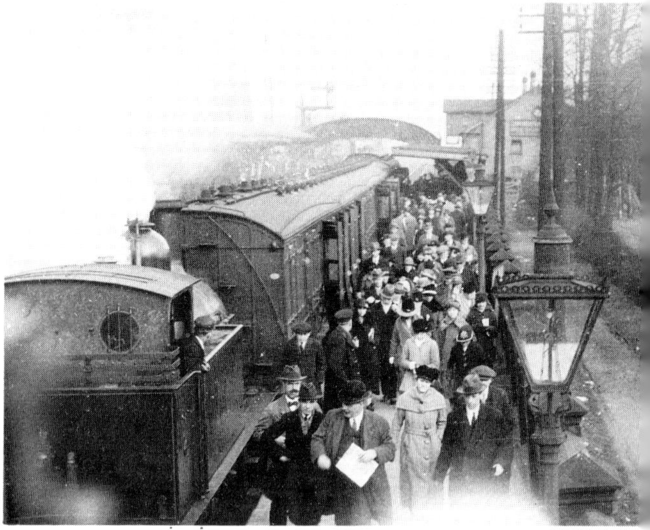

Above:
Where there was no tram service, trains continued to be well patronised until the widespread use of motorbuses, as witnessed here by the arrival at Beeston on 3 February 1920 of the MR's 12.45 'dinner time' train from Nottingham.
NAO/CA.ENQ/1920/17/reproduced by permission of the Principal Archivist

Passenger traffic

In the summer of 1927 the LNER recorded a 59% drop in receipts and a 54% decline in passenger numbers between Nottingham and Ilkeston. This was almost entirely due to the increasing number of motorbuses operating between the city and the outlying suburban districts. By 1927 companies such as Trent Motor Traction, Barton Brothers of Beeston, Tansey & Severn Ltd, Williamsons & Sons and the Midland General Omnibus Co were running extensive local services, as well as seaside excursions.

Within the city the Corporation had rapidly improved its service after the first successful motorbus had started operating on the Bagthorpe and Bentinck Road route from 20 May 1920. By 1928 there were 14 routes, and, three years after the tram service between King Street near the Old Market Square and Vernon Street Basford was replaced by a trolleybus service in April 1927, the Corporation decided to convert all its tram routes to trolleybus operation. On 5 September 1936 the last tram trundled past Nottingham Victoria station to be replaced by a motorbus service to Arnold. By 1939 the Corporation was operating 221 four-wheeled motorbuses and 125 six-wheeled trolleybuses, the majority being double-deckers only a few years old.

Right:
MR 4-2-2 No 664 stands in front of Nottingham Station East signalbox with an express c1924.
T. G. Hepburn/Rail Archive Stephenson

Below right:
Ex-MR 4-4-0 No 408 gathering speed past Lenton South Junction in 1929. Nottingham Castle stands out prominently in the background above the signalbox.
F. W. Stevenson/NCCLSL/ 2103

Bottom:
Photographed about the time of the Grouping, MR 4-4-0s Nos 527 and 1042 prepare to leave the east end of Nottingham station with a St Pancras express.
T. G. Hepburn/Rail Archive Stephenson

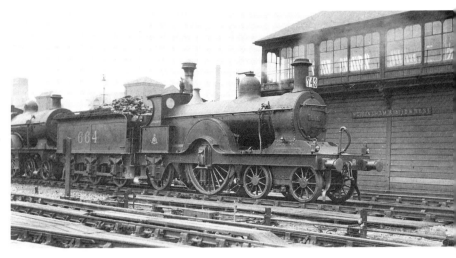

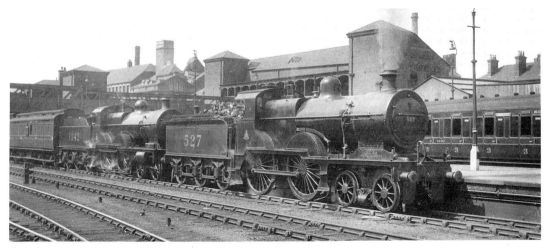

The railways' response was rationalisation, and the late 1920s and early 1930s witnessed severe cutbacks particularly by the LNER. The 1920 survey of passengers using local railway stations (mentioned in the last chapter) had not only shown just how many people used Corporation transport compared with the railways, but how places like Hucknall could not realistically support three stations. Between 7am and 9.30am on 12 January 1920 505 passengers travelled to Nottingham from the MR station, 108 used the GC station but only 53 travelled from the GN station. The obvious solution for the LNER was to close one station in towns served by both the ex-GN and ex-GC, and bearing in mind the 1920 figures the closures were sensibly concentrated on the ex-GN Leen Valley line, Bulwell Forest closing on 23 September 1929, followed on 14 September 1931 by all the remaining stations. The ex-GC did not escape completely, however, and Carrington, which had failed to develop into a suburban station, was closed on 24 September 1929 followed by Bulwell Hall Halt (opened on 24 April 1904) on 5 May 1930.

To the east of the city the Nottingham Suburban line, inherited by the LNER, had already been abandoned by passengers and slipped into a gentle decline. But for a brief period after the partial collapse of Mapperley Tunnel on 23 January 1925 the line found itself coping with all the LNER's coal traffic to and from Colwick yard as well as passenger trains diverted from the 'back line'. Then, on 10 July 1928, the peaceful decay at Sherwood station was shattered again, this time by the arrival of 6,550 children and 284 teachers in 13 special trains from Basford & Bulwell, Thorneywood and Nottingham London Road (Low Level) travelling to join thousands of others in Woodthorpe Park to entertain King George V and Queen Mary before the official opening of University College, Nottingham. But

the renaissance was short-lived and a year and a half later Sherwood signalbox was closed and the whole line singled. The final passenger trains passed over the line on 14 September 1931 when the ex-GN Leen Valley service was withdrawn, after which any direct access to Nottingham Victoria station was made impossible by an alteration to Trent Lane Junction, which surprisingly involved the retention of the Suburban line's double-span bridge.

Despite this simplification of LNER passenger services, the company still had seven stations open for passengers out of a total of 11 within the city boundaries. And although only eight of the 12 platforms at Nottingham Victoria were in normal use, causing J. A. B. Hamilton to comment in the February 1932 edition of the *Railway Magazine* that: 'The station is indeed a good deal more pretentious than its traffic warrants, for there are only about 60 departures from either end daily...' many of these trains to towns also served by the LMS were much faster than their rivals.

For example, most of the 14 local trains which ran to Mansfield via the Mansfield Railway (opened in 1917 from Kirkby South Junction) were faster by 10min than the 17 each way over the LMS's Leen Valley line which took between 37 and 50min from Nottingham. Mansfield (Central) also benefited from the Leeds-Bournemouth expresses as well as a number of through carriages to Marylebone. The LMS was equally hard-pressed to compete in terms of speed with the eight stopping trains to Sheffield and the 14 to Leicester, but managed to run a number of semi-fasts to Newark in a competitive 28min compared with the LNER service of four trains each way via Bottesford Junction which averaged 52min.

Between Nottingham and Derby the LMS ran 28 through trains during the week with 10 on

Right:
A few years later a similar pairing headed by No 554 passes through West Bridgford with the up 'Thames-Forth' express.
T. G. Hepburn/Rail Archive Stephenson

Above:
The first 'Claughton' to find its way to Nottingham caused quite a stir amongst railway enthusiasts, and Gordon Hepburn raced down to what for him was an unusual location to record the occasion in July 1928. *T. G. Hepburn/Rail Archive Stephenson*

Centre left:
M&GN 4-4-0 No 22 in the centre road at Nottingham MR during the 1920s.
T. G. Hepburn/Rail Archive Stephenson

Left:
With the AN&B&EJR's London Road terminus in the background — London Road (Low Level) — LMS 4-4-0 No 722 enters the east end of the LMS station over the Nottingham Canal in the 1920s. *Author's Collection*

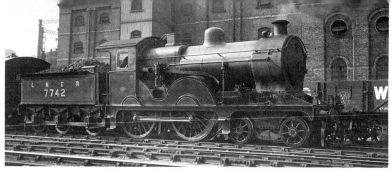

Sundays, and 32 weekday and 13 Sunday return workings, the fastest taking just 23min. From Nottingham Victoria the LNER ran 14 trains out to Derby via Bagthorpe Junction (with 13 return workings and four each way on Sundays) and although the best took 34min and normal journeys occupied between 40 and 45min, the trains were often faster than their LMS 'all stations' counterparts. A journey along the ex-GN Erewash Valley to Pinxton by one of the 10 stopping trains (nine southbound and two each way on Sundays) could take as long, but this service, combined with the LNER's Derby trains, meant Basford & Bulwell station had the benefit of 26 down and 25 up trains every weekday placing it only seven minutes away from the city centre. Similarly, Beeston station on the LMS boasted 55 weekday trains each way because it was served by both Leicester and Derby trains as well as the 16 trains travelling via Long Eaton and along the company's Erewash Valley line terminating variously at Stanton Gate, Ilkeston or Chesterfield. (Some of the Chesterfield trains ran into Ilkeston from the south and out again via the west-north junction.)

Around the LNER's 'back line' via Gedling there were six daily trains usually terminating at Basford & Bulwell, and to Grantham there were 14 trains a day, mostly worked through from Derby, with 15 return workings, (five on Sundays) most stopping at all stations on a 50min journey. A number of services on the 'back line' to and from Basford & Bulwell, and sometimes on to Ilkeston, with others along the Nottingham-Grantham line as far as Radcliffe-on-Trent and on Saturdays to and from Bottesford, were worked by steam railcars. In addition the LNER also ran weekend trains throughout the year to Skegness, Mablethorpe and Sutton-on-Sea for the city's businessmen who had houses there and, during the summer, these were supplemented by numerous excursions to the east coast, a journey to 'Skeggy' taking about two hours.

Nottingham Victoria station might have been 'pretentious' but the ex-GC express services consistently outshone their LMS counterparts. The standard non-stop time to Sheffield was 51min from Nottingham (the fastest taking just 48min) compared with 63min by LMS, and the Leicester trains completed their journeys in between 25 and 27min compared with an average of 40min via Trent. As before the War, the cross-country expresses through Victoria were also unrivalled as the following table reveals:

Southbound

Dep Nottingham	From	To
Weekdays		
12.54am (MX)	York	Bristol
12.36pm	Bradford, Leeds & Newcastle	Bournemouth
1.55pm	Newcastle & Hull	Cardiff & Swansea via Gloucester
5.20pm	Glasgow & Edinburgh	Southampton
8.32pm	Aberdeen & Glasgow	Plymouth & Penzance via Bristol
Sundays		
10.15am	Sheffield	Cardiff & Swansea via Swindon

Northbound

	From	To
Weekdays		
12.30am	Swindon	York
1.0pm	Southampton	Edinburgh & Glasgow
2.12pm	Swansea & Cardiff via Gloucester	Newcastle & Hull
4.51pm	Bournemouth	Newcastle, Leeds & Bradford
9.13pm	Penzance & Plymouth via Trowbridge	Glasgow & Aberdeen
Sundays		
12.30am	Swindon	York
5.48pm	Swansea & Cardiff via Swindon	Sheffield

Above left:
Just after 1.30pm, during the summer of 1924, ex-GN 4-4-2 No 3300 leaves Nottingham Victoria with the down 'Sheffield Pullman'.
T. G. Hepburn/Rail Archive Stephenson

Left:
Ex-GC 4-6-0 No 6164 *Earl Beatty* looks impressive at the head of the Cleethorpes-Leicester train with fish vans at the rear passing through Arkwright Street station in the late 1920s.
T. G. Hepburn/Rail Archive Stephenson

The best cross-country services the LMS could muster were a Lincoln-Bristol restaurant car express and a daily through carriage to Bournemouth which returned on the 2.45pm Bristol-Lincoln working. But apart from the obvious publicity value, did many passengers actually use the LNER through coaches from departure to destination?

When it came to competition for London passenger traffic, the LMS and the LNER were very evenly matched. For a short time between June 1924 and April 1925 the LNER ran the 'Sheffield Pullman' non-stop from Nottingham Victoria to King's Cross via Grantham in 2hr 22min. The train left London at 11.5am reaching Nottingham at 1.28pm, returning from there at 5.38pm and due into King's Cross at 8pm. By 1931 it was still possible to reach King's Cross from Victoria in 2hr 55min by changing trains at Grantham, but the fastest and most frequent services were still along the ex-GC main line or from Nottingham (Midland) to St Pancras via Melton Mowbray. Between Victoria and Marylebone there were eight weekday and three Sunday expresses each way, the fastest up service covering the distance in 2hr 16min. Between Nottingham and St Pancras there were nine southbound and 10 northbound expresses, one down and two up trains taking just 2hr 15min. But of course these were only booked times, and although the LNER ran fewer trains, perhaps it had the better reputation for good timekeeping.

Nevertheless, the booked timings and quality of the LMS's London trains continued to improve right up until the outbreak of War, whilst those over the ex-GC stagnated. The following is a list of the weekday trains in 1939 (excluding services via connections at Grantham):

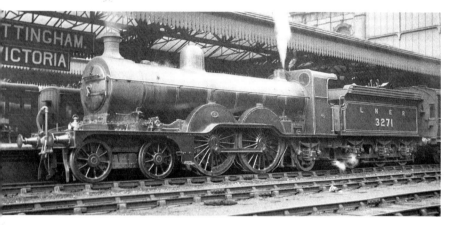

Above left:
Ex-GN Atlantic 4-4-2 No 3271 at Nottingham Victoria in 1928.
J. N. Hall/Rail Archive Stephenson

Left:
Off to school? Travelling from Nottingham Victoria in the 1920s. *NCCLSL*

St Pancras	Marylebone	Nottingham LMS	Nottingham Victoria	
	8.45am		11.32am	2hr 47min
9.5am		11.8am		2hr 3min
10am		12.40pm (via Leicester)		2hr40min
	10am		12.30am	2hr 30min
10.55am		1.44pm		2hr 49min
12 noon		2.40pm (via Leicester)		2hr 40min
	12.15pm		2.58pm	2hr 43min
1pm		3.45pm (via Leicester)		2hr 45min
2.10pm		4.13pm		2hr 3min
	3.20pm		5.36pm	2hr 16min
3.25pm		5.38pm (via Leicester)		2hr 13min
4.30pm		7.17pm (via Leicester)		2hr 47min
	4.55pm		7.11pm	2hr 16min
5pm		7.21pm		2hr 21min
6.20pm		8.23pm		2hr 3min
	6.20pm		8.48pm	2hr 28min
7.50pm		10.22pm (via Leicester)		2hr 32min

Nottingham LMS	Nottingham Victoria	St Pancras	Marylebone	
7am		9.55am (via Leicester)		2hr 55min
	8.21am		10.40am	2hr 19min
8.23am		10.35am		2hr 12min
9.24am		12 noon		2hr 36min
10.14am		12.54pm		2hr 40min
	10.27am		1.10pm	2hr 43min
11.18am		1.21pm		2hr 3min
	12.13pm		2.55pm	2hr 42min
1.25pm		3.32pm (via Leicester)		2hr 7min
2.59pm		5.35pm		2hr 36min
3.42pm		6.25pm (via Leicester)		2hr 43min
	4.21pm		6.38pm	2hr 17min
5.11pm		7.20pm (via Leicester)		2hr 9min
	6.9pm		9pm	2hr 51min
6.40pm		8.55pm		2hr 15min
	7.13pm		9.52pm	2hr 39min

Tickets sales and passenger receipts for the LMS in Nottingham are unfortunately not readily available, but we do have statistics for the LNER. In 1936, for example, 509,701 third-class and 8,075 first-class single and/or return tickets were purchased at Nottingham Victoria station, bringing in £102,422 and £5,796 respectively. In addition 4,224 season tickets were sold for £4,236, and £72,407 was made from parcels traffic.

Freight traffic

By comparison, the LNER's Queen's Walk Goods Department (ex-GC) made £375,754 3s 10d in the same year, illustrating just how important freight traffic remained for the railways between the wars. For example, at night the staff at Colwick yard busied themselves with the express freights to and from Manchester (Deansgate), the 1.50am (SX) departure having started its journey in Liverpool at 4.55pm and due into the capital at 5.32am. But despite this activity and the growth of certain new light industries, the expansion of the Boots Pure Drug Co at Beeston in the 1930s and the sidings to it from the LMS authorised in March 1929 being a notable example, it was the stable heavy mineral traffic which continued to sustain the railway companies around Nottingham between the wars. As certain industries gradually began to rely more on road transport, it was the major railway company yards, unseen by all but the observant rail traveller, that benefited most from what little money there was available for modernisation.

For example, in 1929 it was announced that £100,000 was to be spent improving Beeston

Left:
The three stations at Hucknall in the late 1920s, all views looking north: a. Ex-GN 4-4-2T No 4519 entering the ex-GN station with a train to Nottingham; b. Ex-MR 4-4-0 No 418 waiting at the MR's 1895 station with a Nottingham train; c. Ex-GC 4-4-2T No 6120 entering the 'Central' station with a train bound for the city.
Douglas Thompson/Robert Humm & Co

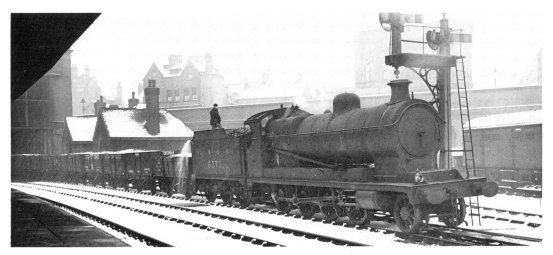

sidings to cope with the increased volume of coal emanating from new collieries in the Dukeries east of Mansfield. The sinking of deep coalmines in this area had started immediately prior to World War 1 and, in 1925, the LMS and LNER had joined forces to build the Mid Nottinghamshire Joint line between Bestwood and Retford to serve the new pits. The only section to open before World War 2 was between Farnsfield and Ollerton in 1931, serving Bilsthorpe colliery sunk by the Stanton Co between 1924 and 1927. Coal from Bilsthorpe, along with that from the new colliery at Blidworth (1926), was, therefore, channelled eastwards along the LMS's single line between Mansfield and Rolleston Junction on the Nottingham-Lincoln branch, the meagre passenger service between Mansfield and Southwell having been withdrawn on 12 August 1929. Between Southwell and Rolleston the line was doubled and a new double line connection was laid to join the Lincoln-Nottingham branch at Fiskerton Junction. Trains could then be worked southwestwards through Nottingham to Beeston sidings, and by 1933 33 were timetabled to make this journey, with 31 returning with empties.

Long distance haulage of coal by both the LNER and LMS was guaranteed during the 1930s by the 'Seven Mile Agreement' whereby collieries in South Yorkshire, Nottinghamshire and Derbyshire restricted the transportation of coal by road to within seven miles of the point of production, an undertaking, according to an LMS report, that the managers '...faithfully honoured'. This protectionism allowed the railways to invest in improvements at Toton and Colwick yards despite coal production having stagnated somewhat in the Erewash and Leen valleys after the General Strike. At Toton new 55ft and 60ft turntables were installed in No 1 and No 2 sheds

in 1926-27, and this was immediately followed by the introduction of 33 2-6-0-0-6-2 Beyer-Garratts between 1927 and 1930, the locomotives taking over the normally double-headed coal trains to Brent. During the summer of 1932 a new mechanical coaling plant capable of discharging 3,000 tons of coal a week was erected along with better ash handling and water softening equipment. By 1934 Toton was employing approximately 1,200 people including 560 in the loco department.

In 1932 the ex-LNWR shed at Colwick closed and the yard and locomotive department became exclusively the domain of the LNER. Four years later £35,000 was spent constructing better locomotive coal handling facilities for the 167 engines shedded there, installing a new 70ft power-operated turntable, a new 260ft ashpit, new water columns and building a new mess and foreman's rooms. Then, in 1938, the gradient in the gravity yard was increased slightly at a cost of £2,600 in order to speed up the sorting of wagons which, by then, had reached a total of over a million a year.

In the summer of 1938, work also began on the mechanisation of the down yard at Toton — the side receiving empty coal wagons for distribution back to the appropriate collieries, as well as loaded iron ore trains. The changes were brought into operation on 30 May 1939, just four months before the outbreak of World War 2. A new reinforced concrete control tower and separate hump room were erected at the end of the high level arrival lines (which crossed the goods and passengers lines through Toton on a bridge at the south end of the yard) where they could co-ordinate the dispersal of wagons into the 18-road 'Meadow sidings' and the 17-road 'north yard'. With mechanisation the shunters' task was reduced to the uncoupling of wagons. The electro-pneumatically operated entry points into the two yards (the 'King', 'Queen', and 'Jack' points) and the colour light signals conveying three indications to the drivers of the diesel shunters propelling wagons over the hump, were operated from the hump room. The choice of route set up in this room and the selection of which sidings the wagons were destined for was printed out automatically in the adjacent control tower from where the points into the sidings and the rail brakes (to control the descent of wagons from the hump) were operated. An illuminated diagram in both the hump room and control tower indicated the position of points, signals and wagons, and in emergencies almost all the functions of the hump room could be carried out from the control tower.

All the sidings in both 'Meadow sidings' and 'north yard' were numbered consecutively from 1 to 35 and classified according to destinations of the wagons. The full list makes interesting reading:

1. Stowage sidings
2. Wait orders
3. Blackwell
4. Common users
5. Kirkby area
6. Kirkby area
7. Swanwick; Brands
8. Pinxton; Langton
9. Riddings; Codnor Park
10. Stanton Gate
11. Cossall; West Hallam, Trowell; Ilkeston
12. Bennerley; Manners
13. Coates Park; New Birchwood; Pye Bridge
14. Heanor Junction
15. Langley Mill & Heanor Town
16. Shipley
17. Sandiacre
18. Cory's works
19. Engine line
20. Toton up sidings
21. End-door wagons
22. Roundwood; Kilnhurst
23. Seymour
24. Summit sidings & Toton loco coal
25. Masborough area
26. Eckington; Birley
27. Treeton
28. Central Division empties
29. Wharncliffe; Wincobank; Chapeltown
30. Avenue
31. Carlton Exchange
32. Clay Cross
33. Carlton Association Collieries
34. Normanton North yard
35. Leeds

Before leaving the 1930s, it is important to mention that the railways did not have a complete monopoly of heavy goods transportation during these years. In 1937 the LNER gained Parliamentary approval to abandon the disused section of Nottingham Canal (inherited from the AN&B&EJR and GN) between Lenton and Eastwood, and lease the remainder of the canal to the Trent Navigation Co for 99 years at an annual rental of £300. At the same time, the River Trent between Nottingham and Newark, operated by the Navigation Co until its transfer to Nottingham Corporation in 1915, was carrying an increasing tonnage to and from the Humber ports. Between the wars, two large transit sheds and two warehouses were built next to Trent Lane, Nottingham, with a rail connection to the LMS, and with the improvement of the river, over 200,000 tons of goods (excluding petrol) were carried annually after 1932. Whilst the railways continued to carry a largely predictable but nevertheless huge quantity of Britain's traditional fuel — coal — the River Trent saw its annual share of petrol carrying increase from just under 5,000 tons in 1928 to 117,500 tons in 1936, and this was the mineral fuelling the growing number of cars, buses and lorries already competing for the railways traffic.

World War 2

As soon as war was declared the LNER Train & Traffic Control Office for the Nottingham District (one of six districts) was evacuated to East Leake. In the following weeks, passenger services throughout the country were severely curtailed. The Midlands was particularly badly affected with the ex-GC main line service cut to only two trains each way daily between Marylebone and Manchester and with their average times increased by almost an hour. This produced journey times far worse than the very first GC expresses in 1899 when the new line was being bedded-in. The LMS also increased the journey times of its expresses, and all passenger trains between Trent and Long Eaton were withdrawn, stations north of Trent on the Erewash Valley line being served only by Nottingham-Chesterfield stopping trains.

It soon became clear that this sort of response to the crisis was not really helping the war effort, and services soon began to normalise. At the end of October 1939 the LMS accelerated its 7.20am and 12.30pm trains from Bradford via Nottingham, and the 4pm return service from St Pancras was retimed to reach Nottingham 32min earlier than under the emergency timetable. Unfortunately, when the LNER introduced its new timetable on 4 December, ex-GC

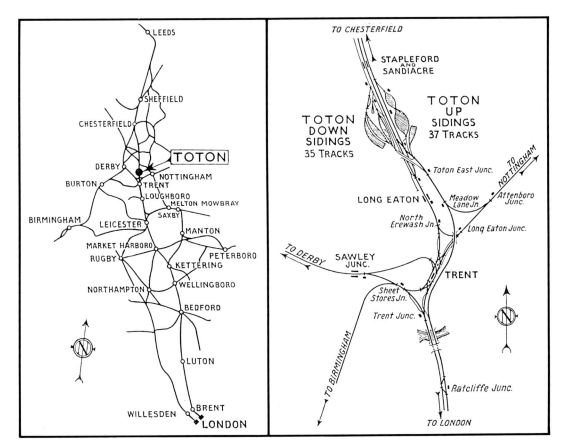

services remained minimal in marked contrast to practically all other trains which were run to prewar schedules, except streamlined and Pullman services which were withdrawn.

Nevertheless numerous extra trains were run for service personnel, freight traffic increased and to deal with the incredible numbers of letters and parcels sent to troops overseas, Nottingham Victoria station became the headquarters of the Army Postal Service, millions of letters, newspapers and parcels and packages being sorted and dispatched during the hostilities. Some of this enormous quantity of paper had to be driven by road to other local stations for loading, whilst parcels were dealt with in the subway under Victoria, which also doubled as an air-raid shelter. A special LNER Army Post Office Mail Train started running between Nottingham and Southampton on 25 April 1944. It was later diverted to Tilbury, then Dover and finally to Folkestone from 16 June1945. When the service was withdrawn on 15 April 1946 it was estimated that the trains had carried over 3 million bags of mail and parcels.

In March 1941 the Nottingham Soroptimist Club opened a canteen for the exclusive use of

HM Forces at the main LMS station, and barely two months later Nottingham suffered its worst bombing raid on the night of 8/9 May 1941 when extensive damage was inflicted to the east and southeast of the city centre and around the railway. The Lace Market was hit, and a number of Boots Co buildings on Island Street and Station Street were gutted. Surprisingly, the LMS station escaped the bombs, refreshment room crockery on platforms Nos 4 and 5 was thrown about, and part of the stable block next to Station Street was demolished. But only a few hundred yards away the LMS carriage sheds and sidings (Eastcroft) received direct hits which razed the wooden sheds to the ground. Twenty-six coaches were completely burnt out and another 71 slightly damaged. Across the line the LNER's London Road (Low Level) goods warehouse also suffered fire damage, and the signalbox had its windows blown out. A little further north the substantial brick ex-LNWR goods warehouse at Manvers Street was almost completely destroyed, losing its roof and top floor, whilst the contents, including a number of box wagons, were consumed in the fire. Part of the ex-Nottingham Suburban Railway embankment

Top:
**On 10 May 1931 LNER
4-6-2 No 4472** *Flying
Scotsman* **and 'Hush-Hush'
4-6-2-2 No 10000 were
exhibited at Nottingham
Victoria, the latter seen at
the buffer stops of platform
No 6 next to a naïve model
of** *Rocket.*
*G. H. F. Atkins/John Marshall
Collection*

Above left:
**Modern Nottingham
stretches out behind ex-GN
4-4-0 No 4329 and 4-4-2T
No 4519 as they negotiate
Bagthorpe Junction with a
train of empty coaching
stock, mainly ex-GN, on
9 August 1932.**
*T. G. Hepburn/Rail Archive
Stephenson*

Left:
**The 12.15 Marylebone-
Manchester express passes
New Basford carriage
sidings on the left behind
LNER 'B17' 4-6-0 No 2834**
Hinchingbrooke **in the
early 1930s.**
*T. G. Hepburn/Rail Archive
Stephenson*

Top:
**LNER 'K3' 2-6-0 No 1164
waits to depart from the
south end of Nottingham
Victoria in the 1930s with a
holiday excursion formed
of the company's green and
cream tourist stock.**
*T. G. Hepburn/Rail Archive
Stephenson*

Above right:
**Platforms Nos 5 and 6 at
Nottingham (Midland)
station looking east with
the ex-GC bridge above in
May 1932.**
*T. G. Hepburn/Rail Archive
Stephenson*

Right:
**LMS 2-8-0 No 8008
carefully manoeuvring
Stanton Ironwork's high-
capacity coke wagons in
Toton up yard on
4 September 1937.** *Hulton
Deutsch Collection
Ltd/Fox 170312*

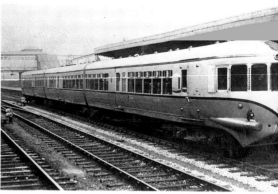

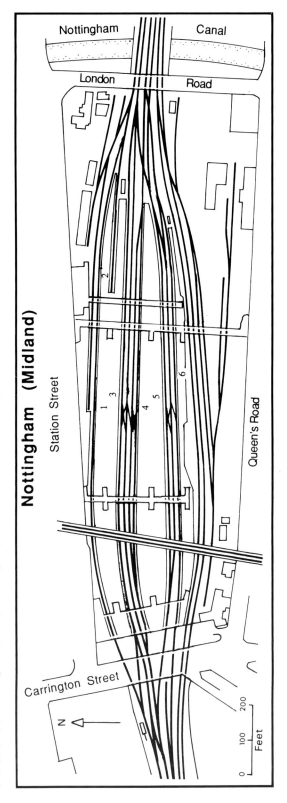

north of the bridge over the ex-MR line was demolished and, tragically, 49 people were killed in the Co-op bakery on Meadow Lane. The factory at Chilwell, once again in the forefront of armaments manufacture and employing over 15,000 people, remained untouched. In all Nottingham suffered 11 air raids during the War but was mercifully spared any others as destructive as those in May 1941.

For Nottingham's young trainspotters, however, there were other diversions as unfamiliar locomotives began to find their way into the area. Two SR 4-4-0s Nos 1156 and 1195 were spotted at Nottingham in December 1941 and, early in 1942, seven ex-Metropolitan Railway tank engines (Class H2) were allocated to Colwick. Although they were reported to be unpopular with local crews, the *Railway Observer* for that year commented: '...One thing, at least, to be said in their favour, is the pleasant tone of the whistle, which is much more cheerful echoing from the hills of the Erewash Valley than the mournful hoot of Mr Stanier's locomotives on the LMS line.'

Another wartime trainspotter recorded SR 'F1' 4-4-0 No 1188, LT&S '2P' 4-4-2T No 2099 and L&Y 0-6-0 No 12123 amongst others shunting at Nottingham and Beeston in the autumn of 1942, and the once proud GN and GC Atlantics also finished their days in the area working local stopping trains, being described by one driver in 1944 as 'hopeless engines'. On 12 May that year the Nottingham-Northampton passenger service was diverted into Nottingham Victoria, leaving London Road (Low Level) station the exclusive domain of the goods department. In June an ex-

LB&SCR Stroudley 0-4-2T, No 2240, was reported shunting at West Hallam station, west of Ilkeston. A few months later at the end of February 1945, as if to illustrate that a return to more certain times was not far off, the clocks on the towers at both Nottingham's main stations were illuminated again. In March, Kirtley's ageing MR 2-4-0 No 20002 (later to be preserved) found its way to Nottingham LMS shed from where it made occasional forays out on local trains, and during Britain's first Summer Bank Holiday weekend after peace had been declared, over 10,000 people passed through the LMS and Victoria stations to take advantage of specials to Llandudno, Torquay, Blackpool, London, Skegness and Mablethorpe.

Above:
The aftermath of the German air raid on Nottingham on 8/9 May 1941. An official LMS photograph taken looking northeast from the carriage sidings in Eastcroft with the LNER yard in the background. *Public Record Office/RAIL421/74*

Right:
The remains of the ex-LNWR Manvers Street goods warehouse after the same air raid, with St Mary's Church in the background. *Public Record Office/RAIL421/74*

9. 1946-62 Nationalisation to Beeching

This is the period in railway history that many still remember with a great deal of nostalgia. Excursions by train to the seaside, or rail tours organised by the RCTS and the SLS created lasting memories. But nostalgia makes it very difficult to come to terms with and understand why the railways changed so suddenly and completely in just a few years after 1962 when such drastic surgery had not seemed necessary before. The numerous photographs taken during the 1950s appear to show an organisation as busy as it was before the War with sidings, warehouses and stations all fully operational. But perhaps it was because this very familiar infrastructure was so solidly intact that any changes, such as a downturn in trade, were difficult to detect. By comparison photographs of the country's roads and the type of vehicles on them in 1946 and 1962, and the sort of new buildings being erected in cities like Nottingham would indicate drastic changes which were not apparent on the railways in the 1950s.

In 1950 there were still 85 working railway horses at Nottingham, although the number had dropped to only eight by 1953 and they were all moved away from the city at the end of July that year. In the mid-1950s, there were still 410 staff employed at the Midland station, dealing with 1.5 million passengers and 2 million parcels a year, and 190 trains daily. Even Trent boasted 63 staff (including 24 signalmen) dealing with the 64 local trains and nine expresses daily which stopped at the station. It would have all been very familiar to an MR employee from the turn of the century.

Between 1946 and 1962 the railways in and around Nottingham changed very slowly and, unfortunately, by so doing and thereby losing ground to road competition, they became obvious targets for Beeching economic cuts after 1962. The 1950s were the years of planning during which time the railways exhibited a deceptive calm before the sudden storm of 'rationalisation' and 'modernisation'.

Passenger services

Passenger services recovered only slowly after the War. On the LMS timekeeping was poor with many trains into and out of Nottingham running between 15 and 30min late, and up trains often an hour late. From March 1947 the 42 LMS Control Districts were reduced to just 20 with Nottingham being allocated its own District Operating Manager. But operating difficulties continued and, to add to the problems, there

Right:
A view looking west from Wilford Road bridge in March 1947 as an ex-MR 4-4-0 negotiates the flood waters. *Nottingham Evening Post/NCCLSL*

was extensive flooding around Nottingham in March 1947 affecting the goods yard and station where the platforms did in reality become islands. On higher ground the LNER attempted to put a little sparkle back into its last independent timetable by applying the title 'The Master Cutler' to the 7.40am from Sheffield to Marylebone, and the 6.15pm return service. A year later the new Eastern Region of British Railways named the 10am from Bradford and the 8.50pm return service 'The South Yorkshireman'. The platform buildings at Nottingham Victoria were steam cleaned during the summer of 1950 which considerably brightened the interior of the station. But the booked timings of London trains were still miserable when compared with prewar schedules, as the following 1949 table shows, and they remained slow throughout the 1950s:

Although there were more timetabled services to and from St Pancras, by the mid-1950s trains through Nottingham Victoria were usually more punctual and, as a result, loyally supported by many Nottingham businessmen. For a few years a certain vitality returned to Nottingham Victoria but, following BR's 1955 Modernisation Plans and with the transfer of the former GC to the LMR on 1 February 1958, it was inevitable that duplicate London services would not continue. In July that year '9F' No 92164 took 'The Master Cutler' from Leicester to Nottingham, start to stop in just under 23min, reaching 86mph near Ruddington. But the feat was very much a final fling as the retreating Eastern Region took the express's title with it, transferring it to a King's Cross-Sheffield Pullman service. Reports of a complete closure of the ex-GC main line then became common despite a major

St Pancras	Marylebone	Nottingham LMR	Nottingham Victoria	
8.50am		11.27am		2hr 37min
	10am		1.4pm	3hr 4min
10.15am		1.33pm (via Leicester)		3hr 18min
11.45am		2.48pm (via Leicester)		3hr 3min
	12.15pm		3.17pm	3hr 2min
12.55pm		4.1pm (via Leicester)		3hr 6min
2pm		4.30pm		2hr 30min
3.12pm		5.45pm		2hr 33min
	3.20pm		6.30pm	3hr 10min
4.50pm		7.29pm (via Leicester)		2hr 39min
	4.50pm (The South Yorkshireman)		7.33pm	2hr 43min
	6.15pm (The Master Cutler)		9.4pm	2hr 49min
6.40pm		9.9pm		2hr 29min

Nottingham LMR	Nottingham Victoria	St Pancras	Marylebone	
6.42am		10am (via Leicester)		3hr 18min
8.31am		11.25am		2hr 54min
	8.43am (The Master Cutler)		11.25am	2hr 42min
9.25am		12.40pm (via Leicester)		3hr 15min
10.17am		1.25pm		3hr 8min
	10.49am		1.58pm	3hr 9min
11.19am		2.10pm		2hr 51min
	12.30pm (The South Yorkshireman)		3.29pm	2hr 59min
1.16pm		4pm (via Leicester)		2hr 44min
	1.46pm		4.28pm	2hr 42min
3.00pm		6.5pm		3hr 5min
4.12pm		7.30pm (via Leicester)		3hr 18min
5.8pm		8.45pm (via Leicester)		3hr 37min
6.8pm		9.20pm		3hr 12min
	6.21pm		9.34pm	3hr 13min
6.58pm		10.55pm (via Leicester)		3hr 57min

Left:
Nottingham Victoria just after World War 2.
Nottingham Evening Post/NCCLSL

rebuilding of the lattice girder bridge over Nottingham Midland station at the end of 1959 and, from 3 January 1960, all expresses were withdrawn and replaced by 'semi-fasts'.

The alternative expresses from Nottingham Midland station remained pedestrian with a trip to London taking as long, or longer than a pre-1914 journey, the fastest train taking 2hr 7min. The introduction of the 'Robin Hood' express at the beginning of February 1959 added a touch of romance to London services, but real improvements started in October 1961 when the prestigious blue 'Midland Pullman' diesel service was introduced between St Pancras and the city, anticipating a significant acceleration of all but the local stopping services when the Midland main line was dieselised from September the following year. The two-hour barrier between Nottingham and London was finally broken, by just one minute on the fastest up journey and by two and a half on the return service which averaged 63.1mph. This perhaps seems almost academic as other trains were not so fast, but these improvements, no matter how small, were significant and began to make up for the loss of the ex-GC expresses.

By comparison, improvements in local stopping services were patchy between 1946 and 1962, the period being characterised by losses of services due to road competition, balanced by some infusion of new stock as the 1955 Modernisation Programme took effect. On 16 June 1947 the Ilkeston Town branch closed to passengers and, although excursions continued to make full use of the ex-GN & LNWR line, the two booked passenger trains each way between Nottingham (Victoria) and Market Harborough were withdrawn from 7 December 1953. This was followed two years later by the withdrawal of the 7.40am Newark Northgate-Nottingham Victoria, and the 5.35pm return working. Then

Above left:
The south end of Nottingham Victoria with ex-GN 4-4-0 No 2194 waiting to leave with a Derby-Grantham train on 12 July 1947. *H. C. Casserley*

Left:
With a varied collection of carriages in tow, LNER 'B1' 4-6-0 No 1141 passes the point where the goods and passenger lines merged just south of the ex-GC's bridge across the Trent on 16 August 1947.
T. G. Hepburn/Rail Archive Stephenson

Left:

Ex-GW 4-6-0 No 6990 *Witherslack Hall* approaching Nottingham Victoria from the south through Arkwright Street station during the Locomotive Exchange Trials on 24 June 1948 with an express to Manchester. This locomotive is currently preserved only a few miles away at Loughborough on the Great Central Railway (1976) plc. *J. P. Wilson*

Below left:

Passengers at Nottingham Midland station anxiously await the arrival of a holiday train in 1949. *F. W. Stevenson*

Bottom:

Nottingham (LMR) MPD seen on 22 August 1948. Ex-MR 0-4-4T still retains its LMS number 1324, whilst 0-6-0 No 43214 behind has already been renumbered into BR stock. *J. F. Henton*

Top:
An unusual visitor to Toton on 12 June 1949: ex-LNER 2-8-0-0-8-2 No 69999 *en route* from the Lickey incline. *J. F. Henton*

Above left:
Weekday Cross Junction looking north from the line to London Road (High Level). Ex-LNER 4-6-0 No E1298 charges out of Parliament Street tunnel with an empty coaching stock train on 10 May 1949. *J. F. Henton*

Left:
Arkwright Street signalbox controlled the north junction into and out of the GC's goods yard. In this official LNER photograph taken during the early months of World War 2, ex-GN 'O2' 2-8-0 No 3483 hauls a train of naval guns out of the yard. *LNER/Ian Allan Library*

Left:
A RCTS special travelling south behind ex-GN 'C12' No 67363 approaches the remains of Sherwood station on the Nottingham Suburban line on 16 June 1951. Four years later the line was dismantled.
G. H. F. Atkins/John Marshall Collection

Bottom:
Toton at night, 1951. *British Railways*

on 17 September 1956 the Annesley 'Dido' which, since the opening of the GC, had taken workers from Bulwell Common and Newstead stations to Annesley shed, was withdrawn and a bus service substituted in its place. Two days later the first BR DMUs in the Nottingham area started working between Nottingham Victoria and Grantham and, on 14 April 1958, others began running between Derby and Lincoln on the former MR line. Because of their superior acceleration, the new units offered a considerably faster all-stations service. A steam-hauled journey between Nottingham and Newark used to take between 40 and 48min, but this was

reduced to only 34min by DMU, and in the summer of 1958 the whole Derby-Lincoln timetable was recast to take advantage of this improvement.

Unfortunately, DMUs did not find their way on to any other local line, and with the closure of Basford Vernon to passengers on 4 January 1960, it could be argued that services like those between Nottingham, Mansfield and Worksop were already being considered for withdrawal.

Freight traffic

On 29 May 1954, over 6,000 employees of Raleigh Industries, Nottingham, travelled in 12 special trains from the city for a day out at Blackpool. By comparison hardly any of the firm's raw materials and very little of their finished products were travelling by rail at this time, the company being already heavily dependent on road transport. The statistics confirming this come from a survey carried out in the mid-1950s when local firms were asked to comment on their use of rail and road transport. The answers in the survey indicate industrial attitudes at a watershed, with some firms remaining loyal to their use of the railways, and others turning wholeheartedly to road haulage. What is noticeable, however, was no matter what their preferences, most firms criticised the railways for their high charges, their unreliability and the problems caused by the inevitable transhipment of loads, which judging from the comments often lead to breakages and damage. One firm remarked that it was only economical to use the railway for journeys over 120 miles from their factory. Another firm, Richard Sankey & Son Ltd of Bulwell which made red clay flowerpots and had moved its business in 1892 to take advantage of a private railway siding, commented that from using the railway 100% in 1925, by 1950 it no longer used the railway at all, its raw mate-

rial including coal, coming in by road. Surprisingly, many lace firms still sent their goods by rail but, generally speaking, it was heavy industry that continued to rely on the railways, with the help of government incentives.

Following the nationalisation of the mines and the railways, government money was available for a massive investment in the coal industry, and at the beginning of 1948 plans were unveiled for the 'mechanisation' of the up yard at Toton — which dealt with loaded coal wagons — in effect completing the modernisation started before the War. The rebuilding was thorough. Sixteen miles of track was removed, the site relevelled and 27 miles of new track re-layed. Four brick signalboxes replaced the former MR cabins on the main line, and a reinforced concrete control tower and hump room replaced the numerous shunters' cabins. According to contemporary accounts, as with the 1939 improvements, all alterations were achieved with minimal disruption to traffic, the final stage being brought in to use on 4 September 1950. At the end of 1951, the *Railway Gazette* lavished considerable space in describing the alterations, the route setting, rail brakes and special colour light signalling, the loudspeaker system and electric lighting, but what really gave the true picture of Toton's importance in traffic terms was the classification of its 37 new sidings:

WEST SIDE
Fan 1
1. Long Eaton
2. Foleshill Gasworks
3. Birmingham, Windsor Street Gasworks
4. Western Region via Gloucester
5. Westerleigh, Bristol
6. via Wichnor, excluding Stafford & Salop
7. Derby St Mary's, Ripley & Wirksworth branches and stations to Darley Dale
8. Chaddeston, Water Orton & NS line

Fan 2
9. Holwell
10. Birmingham, Nechells Gasworks
11. Washwood Heath, front fan
12. Beeston
13. Washwood Heath, back fan
14. via Banbury
15. via Bordesley
16. Birmingham, Saltley Gasworks
17. Burton & Exchange
18. Branston Exchange

EAST SIDE
Fan 3
19. District wagon repair shop

20. Eastern Region via Nottingham
21. Lloyds, Weldon & Corby
22. Leicester Exchange
23. Leicester Humberstone Road
24. Leicester Aylestone Road Gasworks
25. Wigston, including KI coke
26. Toton Down Yard
27. Kettering Exchange, excluding KI coke
28. Wellingborough

Fan 4
29. Lillie Bridge
30. Bletchley Exchange
31. Rugby Exchange
32. Northampton Exchange
33. Watford Exchange
34. Willesden High Level
35. Willesden Low Level
36. Chilwell group for subsidiary shunting
37. Eastern Region, via Peterborough

Almost exactly two years after work at Toton had been finished, the nationalised railways and mines worked in tandem again to complete another unfinished prewar project and, on 24 September 1952, Lord Feathers, Secretary of State for the Co-ordination of Transport, Fuel & Power, opened a 7½-mile long branch from both the former MR and GN's Leen Valley lines at Bestwood Park Junction and Calverton Branch Junction respectively, northeastwards to Calverton Colliery, the first new pit to open since nationalisation. The formation allowed for double track, and there were new signalboxes at Bestwood Park Junction (55 levers), Calverton Branch Junction (35 levers), Papplewick Junction (40 levers) and Calverton Colliery (10 levers).

Then, at the end of the decade, when a new electricity generating power station was planned for a site at Holme Pierrepont just south of Colwick, a two-mile long branch from the Nottingham-Grantham line immediately south of the River Trent was constructed to a new colliery at Cotgrave, involving the erection of a long sweeping concrete viaduct at Radcliffe-on-Trent and a double span steel bridge across the Nottingham-Grantham road (A52) by then already a dual carriageway.

But perhaps all this development was over-optimistic. By the mid-1950s the Calverton colliery branch had been singled and signalboxes boarded up and, after considerable opposition, the power station at Holme Pierrepont was not built. By the early 1960s railway freight generally was declining rapidly. For a brief period after their allocation to the Eastern Region in December 1957, the '9Fs' working the 31 daily

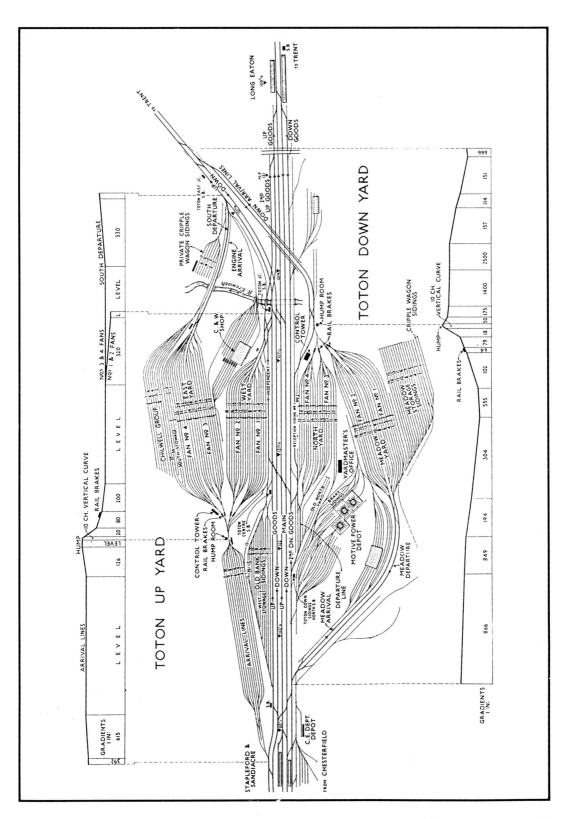

Left:
Radford Junction's splitting distant at Lenton indicates to the driver of ex-LMS 2-6-0 No 43033 that the line is set for the 5.12pm from Nottingham to take the ex-MR Leen Valley line towards Mansfield on 22 August 1952. *J. P. Wilson*

Below left:
Ex-MR 4-4-0 No 41082 has seen better days as it makes a smoky exit from Nottingham Midland under London Road bridge with a lunchtime train to Lowdham on the Lincoln line on 10 April 1952. *J. F. Henton*

Bottom:
Trent North Junction with ex-LMS 0-6-0 No 44084 hauling an up coal train on 10 May 1952. *J. F. Henton*

Above left:
The 'old' coaling stage at Nottingham MPD on 6 April 1953, with ex-MR 0-4-4 No 58085 (one of the last locomotives to work the 'Southwell Paddy').
J. F. Henton

Above:
The booking hall at Nottingham Victoria being decorated in May 1953 ready for the Coronation of HM Queen Elizabeth II. *IAL*

Centre left:
Ex-LNER 'B1' 4-6-0 No 61315 pulls away from Nottingham Victoria and enters Sherwood Rise Tunnel with the 1.55pm service to Chesterfield on 28 October 1952.
J. F. Henton/NRM

Left:
Dismantling of the ex-Nottingham Suburban Railway's up line bridge over the ex-GN line at Sneinton had already begun as ex-GN 'J6' 0-6-0 No 64320 heads eastwards out of Nottingham with a Grantham train on 2 August 1954. The down connection was immediately behind the locomotive, and the bridge over the ex-MR Lincoln line was in the background just between the two carriages. *J. F. Henton/NRM*

Right:
The grandeur of Nottingham Victoria station at night, with ex-LNER 4-6-0 'B1' No 61376 heading north on 29 October 1954. *R. H. Rogers*

Below right:
Ex-GN 0-6-0 No 64273 entering Basford North (originally Basford & Bulwell) station from the east. The former GC & GN Joint connection to the ex-GC main line at Bulwell South Junction branches off to the left, whilst behind the train beyond the road bridge, separate up and down lines curve to the right to link up with the ex-GC at Bagthorpe Junction. *T. G. Hepburn/Rail Archive Stephenson*

Bottom:
The signal at Basford North station indicates that the route is set for ex-LNER 'B1' 4-6-0 No 61188 to take the 'back line' through Daybrook and Colwick, avoiding Nottingham with this 1950s holiday excursion.
T. G. Hepburn/Rail Archive Stephenson

Annesley-Woodford fast freights — the 'Windcutters' — confirmed the enviable reputation of this particular freight service introduced on 30 June 1947, and as Colin Walker commented in his evocative book, *Main Line Lament*: 'The sight of their ten-coupled driving wheels racing round and the exhaust 'frothing' above their smoke-boxes before falling behind in a trail as long as their rattling, bouncing trains, was quite unforgettable.' But the success of these trains was not sustained after the LMR take-over.

Decline was also easy to detect at Colwick, where, in July 1959, 68,653 wagons were handled, compared with 89,815 in July 1957. The figures were still significant but, during repairs to Mapperley Tunnel in 1959, which caused widespread disruption to freight traffic, it was suggested Colwick could be closed altogether. This argument was given further force when Mapperley Tunnel had to be abandoned completely on 4 April 1960 after a serious collapse, which effectively isolated Colwick yard from the collieries of the Leen Valley. Thirty-nine down and 37 up trains daily had to be rerouted through Nottingham Victoria, Weekday Cross and Trent Lane junctions to enter the yard from the west, increasing operating costs and reducing the number of wagons handled to only 50,297 in July that year. At the same time Daybrook and Gedling stations were closed to passengers and a substitute bus service laid on.

These problems coincided with and undoubtedly hastened the end of the steam-hauled loose-coupled mineral train. Early in September 1955 Toton's first '9F', No 92051, arrived, and by May 1958 all the ex-LMS Garratts had gone; Toton lost its last pair, Nos 47987/95, the previous year. By 1958 there were already 15 diesel shunters at Toton and, at the beginning of 1960, facilities for the new main line diesels were being provided there. In October two new 200hp Drewry shunters, Nos D2300/1, were allocated to Colwick and then, at the beginning of 1962, the first eight new 'Peaks', Nos D1-5/7/9/10, were allocated to Toton, followed in May that year by Nos D140/5/9/52/8. On 7 May full diesel working started to Castle Donington power station, as well as on the Toton-Wichnor and Toton-Washwood Heath freights, and with the introduction of the new passenger timetable in September 1962, most main line trains around Nottingham became diesel-hauled.

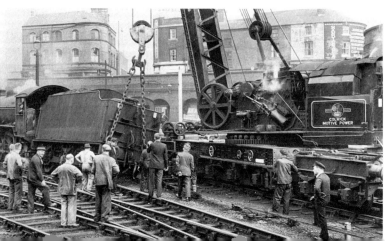

Above left:
Off to the seaside! The crowded platforms at Nottingham Victoria in July 1957, only 10 years before the station was demolished.
Nottingham Evening Post

Left:
A slight mishap at Nottingham Victoria on 15 September 1961 brings the Colwick 36-ton steam crane into action.
Nottingham Evening Post

10. 1963-69 Rationalisation

In these six years the railways in and around Nottingham changed almost beyond recognition: five lines and 34 local stations were closed, Nottingham Victoria (excepting the clock tower) was razed to the ground, over a hundred manual signalboxes were made redundant, diesel traction replaced steam completely, and, apart from the frequency and the speed of trains, the passenger service was cut back to the pattern it had been one hundred years previously. Rationalisation seemed unstoppable and, to all but the old guard or a few of those with radical new ideas, inevitable.

The first line to close in this period was the ex-GN Erewash Valley line to Pinxton on 5 January 1963. After that, piecemeal closures gave way to planned wholesale rationalisation following the publication on 27 March that year of Dr Beeching's *The Reshaping of British Railways* report. By 1969 all but one of his recommendations listed below had been carried into effect.

Passenger services to be withdrawn:

- York-Sheffield Victoria-Nottingham Victoria-Leicester Central-Banbury
- Nottingham Midland-Leicester London Road (local)
- Nottingham Midland-Melton Mowbray-Kettering
- Nottingham Midland-Melton Mowbray (local)

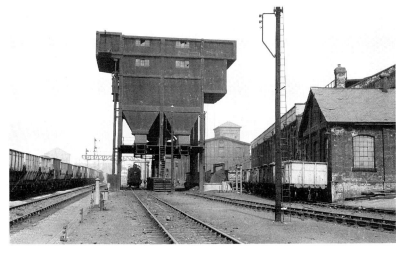

Left:
Nottingham's impressive, but ugly, concrete coaling tower photographed on 26 June 1964. To the right is No 3 Shed and to the left the goods lines running towards Nottingham Midland station in the background.
R. J. Essery

Below left:
Bestwood Park Junction on the ex-MR Leen Valley line looking northeast on 18 August 1962 with ex-LMS 4-6-0 No 45270 passing with an excursion from Blackpool. This was the junction for both Bestwood colliery and the post-World War 2 Calverton colliery. The stone bridge immediately behind the locomotive originally carried the road across the line to Moorbridge Cottages.
J. Cupit

105

- Nottingham Victoria-Derby Friargate (ex-GN Derbyshire Extension line)
- Nottingham Midland-Trent-Derby Midland (local)
- Nottingham Midland-Worksop (ex-MR Leen Valley line)
- Nottingham Victoria-Leicester Central-London Marylebone
- Nottingham Midland-Lincoln St Marks
- Nottingham Midland-Sheffield Midland (local)

Passenger services to be modified:

- Nottingham Midland-Leicester London Road-Birmingham New Street
- Nottingham Midland-Derby Midland
- Nottingham Midland-London St Pancras
- Nottingham-Grantham

Stations to be closed

(in the area south of Alfreton and Kirkby-in-Ashfield, west of Burton Joyce and Radcliffe-on-Trent, north of Edwalton, Ruddington and Trent and East of Ilkeston [GN]):

Alfreton & South Normanton (MR)
Awsworth (GN)
Basford & Bulwell (Basford North) (GN)
Bulwell (Market) (MR)
Burton Joyce (MR)
Carlton & Netherfield (MR)
Codnor Park & Ironville (MR)
Hucknall (Byron) (MR)
Ilkeston (North) (GN)
Ilkeston Junction & Cossall (MR)
Kimberley (East) (GN)
Langley Mill & Eastwood (MR)
Linby (MR)
Long Eaton (MR)
New Basford (GC)
Newstead (MR)
Nottingham Victoria (GC & GN)
Pye Bridge (MR)
Radford (MR)
Stanton Gate (MR)
Stapleford & Sandiacre (MR)
Trowell (MR)
Trent (MR)

Bulwell Common (GC), Hucknall Central (GC), and Nottingham Arkwright Street (GC) had been scheduled for closure before the publication of the report, but for some reason Nottingham London Road (High Level) (GN) was not mentioned in the original Beeching list and, although outside the area of this book, it is relevant to add that Skegness, Newark Castle and both Mansfield Town and Woodhouses stations were listed for closure, which would leave the latter town with no passenger service at all.

The maps accompanying the report confirmed the importance of the ex-MR's Erewash Valley line as a freight artery, little affected by the move away from wagon loads and traffic generated from small private sidings. But it was proposals for cut backs in passenger facilities which hit the headlines. The whole front page of the *Nottingham Evening Post* on Wednesday 27 March, the date of the report's publication, was taken up with the story, although it was only in the inside pages that any attempt was made to quantify the impact locally. At a press conference a local reporter asked Dr Beeching whether he agreed that Nottingham was the worst affected city in the country and with the loss of through services would end up at the end of two branch lines. Beeching would not be drawn, remarking that he had not singled out Nottingham for special attention.

Local reaction to the report was mixed. Passengers and railway enthusiasts were against the cuts, but just before Bulwell Common station closed earlier that month, the stationmaster there was reported as having said: 'If I had three passengers a day on average during the winter, I was doing well. No one would run a business on such an understanding as that, and it will be no tragedy, so far as this station is concerned, that the passenger facilities have been withdrawn.' Nevertheless, in April, Sandiacre Parish Council and the Stapleford Ward Labour Party voiced their objections to the Beeching Report and Lord Lanesborough, president of the Great Central Railway Association, announced his plans to keep the line open. Nottingham Chamber of Commerce thought the report was a 'brilliant analysis' but its implementation might cause hardship. Nottingham's three Conservative MPs supported the plans, but the MPs for Ashfield, Mansfield, Bassetlaw, Ilkeston and North-East Derbyshire recorded their opposition and, with a general election on the horizon, William Whitlock, Labour MP for North Nottingham, commented heroically: 'I warn the Minister of Transport that if he operates this plan, in Nottingham and Nottinghamshire, he will be hated even more than is the wicked Sheriff of Nottingham.'

Whether for or against, however, it is clear that many saw the Beeching plans as an inevitable stage in the modernisation of the urban environment. It has to be remembered

Left:
The 'back', or east side of Nottingham Victoria, showing the entrance to the public thoroughfare across the station between Glasshouse Street and Milton Street in November 1963. *Nottingham Evening Post*

Below left:
Following the closure of Mapperley Tunnel in April 1960, all coal trains to and from Colwick yard were diverted through Nottingham Victoria. Here ex-LNER 2-8-0 No 63878 makes its way south passed Weekday Cross Junction. The open bus station is now the site of the Broad Marsh Shopping Centre. *C. P. Walker*

Bottom:
Ex-LMS '8F' 2-8-0 No 48304 makes a fine sight leaving Sherwood Rise Tunnel in the evening of 29 July 1963 with a Woodford-Annesley train of empty coal wagons. *T. Boustead*

Left:
A photograph taken from the station bridge at Bulwell Common looking north as BR '9F' 2-10-0 No 92073 heads towards Nottingham with an up freight. Disappearing behind the signalbox is the single down line to Bestwood Junction on the ex-GN Leen Valley line and, behind the box wagons in the centre of the train, the cutting for the up line from Bestwood can just be made out. *T. G. Hepburn/Rail Archive Stephenson*

Below left:
Travelling due east, ex-LMS '8F' No 48395 trundles past the Beeston Boiler Co's works and sidings on 18 March 1964. The siding leaving the up goods line on the left served the Boots Co factories. *K. Bale*

Bottom:
At 7.18 in the morning of 9 May 1964, ex-LMS 4-6-2 No 46251 *City of Nottingham* waits at Nottingham Victoria to take a RCTS special to Eastleigh and Swindon. This was only the second, and last, time this locomotive came to the city whose name it carried. *J. F. Henton/National Railway Museum*

Right:
Most of the sidings at
Colwick are shown in this
photograph taken on
29 May 1964 looking north.
In the foreground is the
ex-LNWR shed with North
Western Terrace behind,
and above these buildings
the far larger ex-GN range
of locomotive sheds. At the
top of the picture the ex-GN
Derbyshire & North
Staffordshire Extension
lines leading to Gedling (the
'back line') crosses the
ex-MR line between
Nottingham and Lincoln via
Newark. *Cambridge
University Collection of Air
Photographs: copyright
reserved*

Bottom
Nottingham Victoria South
signalbox c1965 with half
the 95 levers of the Railway
Signalling Co frame
showing. The block shelf had
hardly altered in over 60
years; only two of the
instruments shown are not of
GC origin. *D. J. Powell*

that during the 1960s almost every town in the country undertook some form of redevelopment and still has the scars to prove it. The private motorcar, the embodiment of personal choice, had to be accommodated at all costs, and the building of new roads and car parks went hand-in-hand with wholesale demolition and redevelopment in cities like Nottingham. In April 1963 the £1 million contract to build the M1 motorway bridge over the Trent near Long Eaton was awarded to Brims & Co Ltd of Newcastle, and in the same month the Minister of Transport, Ernest Marples, approved Nottingham's £1.5 million inner road scheme, the construction of which would cause more upheaval than the building of the GC main line 65 years before. In July a new city architect was appointed by the Corporation who considered its development plans out of date and looked for fundamental and large scale changes to the city. If Victoria station and the GC were monuments to a Victorian ideal, then the dual carriageway of Maid Marian Way and the buildings which surround it are the 1960s equivalent. In September plans were unveiled to erect a 16-storey block of flats on the site of Sherwood station, and the following month the Chairman of the Housing Committee commented that he hoped to be able to build more such housing on station sites made redundant in the Beeching report.

Any concerted opposition to the report was hampered by the provisions of the 1962 Transport Act which allowed only individual cases of hardship to be used as evidence for the retention of passenger services. Nevertheless, there were campaigns to try and co-ordinate opposition which seems to have been strongest in Lincolnshire. There the railways had made seaside resorts like Mablethorpe and Skegness ('Nottingham-on-Sea'), and the loss of the many annual

excursions from the Midlands which were still well patronised was enough to convince Nottingham Corporation in May 1963 to support protests against the withdrawal of the service to Skegness.

A total of 138 protests were lodged against the withdrawal of the passenger service between Nottingham Victoria and Derby Friargate but, by February 1964, rumours were circulating that the site of Victoria had already been sold for £3 million. As far as the clock on the station tower at Victoria was concerned it was all over, its hands having stopped at 12 o'clock the previous summer. The withdrawal of the passenger service was confirmed at the end of June 1964 and, at 10.30pm on Saturday 5 September, the last regular passenger train left Victoria for Derby. Withdrawal of the passenger service between Nottingham Midland and Worksop over the ex-MR Leen Valley line was announced in November 1963 and, on 12 October 1964, all stations on that line were closed to passengers. Stations along the ex-MR Erewash Valley line (with the exception of Trent) lingered on a little longer until closure on 2 January 1967.

The only survivors in the face of these relentless closures, were the stations on the ex-MR line to Newark Castle and Lincoln St Marks, which were reprieved in November 1964. A junction was then installed between that line and the ex-GN just west of Netherfield & Colwick station nearly 100 years after the previous one on this site had been taken out of use. Grantham trains could then be run into Nottingham Midland station and thoughts could turn again to the closure of Colwick yard, thereby concentrating the flow of coal, iron ore and other freight through Toton. Considering how simple this connection was to install, and how time-consuming it had been to exchange trains

Above:
By the time this photograph was taken on 9 July 1966 steam-hauled passenger trains were becoming rare. This Saturdays only Bradford-Poole working did, however, invariably produce an ex-LMS 'Jubilee' as seen here with No 45562 *Alberta* approaching Nottingham from the west. Some of the ex-MR wooden sheds in the background look well past their best. *J. Cupit*

Right:
'Wild ones invade seaside — 90 arrests', proclaims the headline of the *Daily Mirror* read by one of these two young women apparently waiting for a Skegness train at Nottingham Victoria on 30 March 1964. Wild ones at 'Skeggy'? *Nottingham Evening Post*

Left:
The two little girls seem unconcerned as BR '9F' 2-10-0 No 92089 storms northwards through the remains of Carrington station on 3 September 1902 with an Annesley freight. *John Marshall*

through the junctions at Sneinton, especially excursions, it seems unbelievable that BR had taken so long to achieve it. Unfortunately, as R. T. Munns, BR Liaison Officer with the NCB and CEGB, pointed out it should have been the ex-MR line between Netherfield and Sneinton that was abandoned instead of the ex-GN line, as Colwick Road, Trent Lane and Meadow Road level crossings could have been eliminated on the former route. It is indeed tempting to believe that the MR's successor, the LMR, still felt it had to vanquish the AN&B&ECJR intruder and that this, somehow, explains why it took two years before Grantham trains were sensibly run into the Midland station over the new connection.

The LMR tightened its control in Nottingham from 3 January 1966 when the former Leicester and Nottingham Districts were amalgamated to form an East Midlands Division with headquarters at BR's new Furlong House, Nottingham, built next to the Nottingham MPD. At the same time the Regional boundary was extended to incorporate Colwick, the MPD soon finding its 'O1' and 'O4' 2-8-0s replaced by Stanier '8Fs' and 'Black 5s'. But steam was already giving way to diesel traction, with the steam shed at Nottingham having closed on 15 April 1965 (although diesels continued to be stabled there until 21 November 1966), and Toton rapidly becoming the main diesel depot for the region. By then over 100 diesels were being maintained there with only a handful of steam locomotives, crews beginning to work 'out & home' diesel-hauled goods runs to Wellingborough, Birmingham and Northampton, returning from the latter with Willesden freights. The new Toton diesel depot boasted all the latest equipment to handle category 'A' exams, with 15 roads, three of which had four-ton overhead cranes for the lifting of engines and heating boilers. There were wheel profiling facilities, as well as a 3,000hp capacity Creswell static load resistor for the testing of power units at full load. The depot also provided administrative back-up for the 50-odd supervisors, inspectors, clerks, and over 300 artisan staff, as well as training facilities and the other necessary amenities to serve 400 maintenance staff, 400 footplatemen and apprentices. The transition from steam to diesel technology seems to have been achieved efficiently and with a high degree of commitment from all personnel, and E. L. Cornwell, writing in *Modern Railways* April 1968, was most impressed with the organisation at Toton and the dedication of the staff there.

Dieselisation, along with electrification, led to fundamental changes in the new LMR timetable introduced on 18 April 1966, trains between London and Manchester being concentrated on the recently electrified West Coast main line, and the opportunity then being taken to recast all diesel-hauled services along the Midland main line. The 'Midland Pullman' was withdrawn, and only one weekday train each way between St Pancras and Nottingham continued to use the route via Melton Mowbray. Unfortunately, this meant the reversal of most expresses in Nottingham with the inevitable increase in through journey times, and speed was also sacrificed for regularity with no train taking less than two hours between the cities. The run down of the ex-GC main line continued when, on 4 September, the three semi-fasts, as well as the York-Poole, Manchester-Marylebone, York-Bristol and Sheffield-Swindon trains, and the two down newspaper and the up Nottingham-Marylebone parcels trains were withdrawn. To all intents and purposes the line north of Nottingham was rendered redundant and on the

following day a token six DMUs each way began to operate between Nottingham Victoria and Rugby Central.

Victoria station soon became a desolate place, with only the freights, DMUs and specials to keep it feeling busy. On 13 August 1966, for example, 'West Country' *Salisbury* No 34002 headed a special between Waterloo and Nottingham, followed on 3 September by 'Merchant Navy' *Elder Dempster Lines* No 35030. Then, on 1 July 1967, Grantham trains were routed into Nottingham Midland, the first time since 1857 and, at 5.34pm on 2 September, the last DMU left Victoria for Rugby. Ten days later the demolition contractors moved in and, by March the following year, only the clock tower remained. With the loss of Nottingham Victoria, Arkwright Street station was reopened to accommodate the Rugby shuttle service until that too ended on 3 May 1969.

The pressure to redevelop Victoria had been great. Only a year after the closure was proposed in Beeching's report, the local *Guardian Journal* had published rumours that a £15 million development project was already being considered for the site. At a meeting of the Notts & District Trades Council on 10 February 1965, Prof Hondelink, a respected transport expert and opponent of Beeching's misleading and one-sided statistical approach to railway problems, pressed for the station to be retained with any new development over the tracks as at New York's Central Station. But his lone voice was not heeded and on 4 June 1965 Notts Planning Committee approved Capital & Counties Property Co plans for a £15 million shopping complex on the site, with 700 flats, a new bus station, new cen-

Left:
After Nottingham Victoria closed, DMUs between Nottingham and Rugby ran from Arkwright Street until 3 May 1969 when the ex-GC line south of the city closed to passenger traffic. Here one of those trains crosses the River Trent at Wilford.
T. G. Hepburn/Rail Archive Stephenson

tral market, 500 seat concert hall, 1,000-seat cinema, bowling alley and 2,800 space car park.

The Victoria Shopping Centre when it was built was not quite so ambitious, but all hopes of retaining a token two tracks beneath the concrete were completely lost in the rush to accommodate Nottingham's motorists. The city planners of the 1960s had no ideas for Rapid Transit networks; in fact they were only too pleased to see the trolleybuses disappear on 30 June 1966. The nearest Nottingham ever came to 'Rapid Transit' was in miniature, when, in 1962, Paul Ritter, architect and lecturer at the School of Art, exhibited a model of the city as he thought it might be in the year 2060 including an underground railway running from Victoria to London Road (High Level) station with stations at Thurland Street, Byard Lane and Broad Marsh. There is little doubt that today's planners would have been briefed to retain some, if not all, of Nottingham Victoria, and could have imaginatively converted it into shopping centre, car park and station.

As the passenger services disappeared in the 1960s, so too did the familiar railway infrastructure. The steam shed at Colwick closed at the beginning of December 1966. Radford and Wollaton collieries closed in 1965 followed two years later by the mine at Bestwood. In the summer of 1968 Clifton colliery closed, and at the end of the year coal trains were routed away from the ex-GN Leen Valley. On New Year's Day 1968 Trent station closed but, as the station came down, Trent power signalbox went up, the contract to equip it having been awarded to AEI-GRS at the end of 1966 as part of a £9.2 million resignalling scheme with similar power boxes at Derby and Saltley. There was the inevitable track rationalisation involving the removal of the Sawley Junction-Trent connection, and the realignment of the through lines there; the severing of the line to Melton Mowbray at London Road Junction, Nottingham, and the lifting of the up and down goods lines through the station with the line through platform No 6 becoming the up goods and the remaining four lines west of the station being redesignated. Between 10pm on 6 December and 5am on 8 December 1969, the station was closed completely to allow for the necessary alterations to be carried out, most of the mechanical signalboxes becoming redundant, including the two built into the station platform buildings. Another sad loss from a historical point of view, were the semaphore sig-

Right:
The new colour light signals are in place but not yet in use as the 15.25 DMU to Lincoln leaves Nottingham Midland on 3 May 1969.
R. W. Sheppard/National Railway Museum

Below right:
Nottingham Station West signalbox, opened in October 1902, has only a few months left as No D33 emerges from beneath Carrington Street.
T. G. Hepburn/Rail Archive Stephenson

Below left and right:
No reclamation of 'architectural' building material here as Nottingham Victoria station comes down in the summer of 1967. *T. G. Hepburn/Rail Archive Stephenson*

nals many of which were MR lower quadrants with wooden arms on wooden posts, most of which were concentrated around Trent junction. Did any survive? By the end of the year the resignalling work was largely complete, the new power box at Trent, the largest on the LMR, then controlling 209 miles of track including 74 route-miles, and dealing with about 250 passenger trains and considerably more coal and freight trains daily.

To traditional railwaymen (those who were left) the resulting track layout around Nottingham must have looked anorexic, and as the culmination of such drastic changes between 1963 and 1969, it must have been difficult to believe that any progress had been achieved during those years. There was some. In May 1967 £9,000 had been spent on providing Nottingham Midland with a new enquiry office, replacing '...the Dickensian atmosphere...' to quote the *Nottingham Guardian Journal* '...(with) modern decor, including potted plants and comfortable chairs for customers.' And armed with the correct information it was then possible after the introduction of the LMR's 1968-69 timetable to travel once again between Nottingham and London in less than two hours even with a stop at Leicester.

But travelling north was not so swift with trains taking between seven and 11min longer than before due to continuing mining subsidence problems on the Erewash Valley line. Ironically, much of this offending coal, when extracted, found its way on to the surface of the valley and into Toton yard, which busier than it had been for years due to the closure of other yards and the run down of Colwick, continued to hump shunt between 3,000 and 4,000 wagons a day. Beeching's aim had been to eliminate this sort of work but, locally, only Ratcliffe power station was able to cope with the new 'Merry-go-round' coal trains by the end of 1969. However, another of Beeching's protégés had emerged fully fledged in the form of Nottingham's Freightliner terminal opened on the site of Beeston sidings on 30 June 1969. Equipped with two 30-ton capacity mobile cranes, its first trains were dispatched nightly to London (York Way) and, from 7 July that year, to Stockton-on-Tees and Newcastle. One of the first customers of the new services was the National Carbonising Co Ltd, which used the London trains to transport its locally produced 'Rexco' smokeless fuel.

But, despite these fruits of modernisation, it could be argued that, by 1969, Nottingham no longer warranted the title of 'rail centre', having lost not only all but one of its city stations, but also two main line through routes between London and the north, and many other cross-country services. The site of Edward Parry's grand central station had been transformed into a shopping centre and car park, and although none of the articles in *Modern Railways* admitted it at the time, Nottingham had become in reality the focal point of just three branch lines.

Left:
From London Road Bridge looking west towards the station, Class 46 No D159 pulls away from platform No 1 with empty coaching stock from a St Pancras train on the 8 July 1969.
J. H. Cooper-Smith

11. 1970 onwards: The Modern Era

The 1970s opened with the erection of another massive shopping complex, the Broad Marsh Shopping Centre, severing Carrington Street and Nottingham station from Listergate and the city centre. The new complex included a covered bus station which opened on 31 October 1971 giving bus and coach passengers a direct and welcoming route into the centre and the semi-pedestrianised area beyond. Passengers arriving in the city by train, however, had to cross the five-lane Canal Street which had become part of Nottingham's racetrack inner ring road, and then negotiate an uninviting subway beneath Collin Street before emerging into the city centre. There is no more tangible evidence of the extent to which Nottingham had turned its back on the railways during the planning years of the 1960s than the Victoria and Broad Marsh Shopping centres, officially opened on 16 March 1973 and 25 March 1975 respectively.

By then a certain calm had returned to the city, and the 1970s witnessed few radical changes to either the railway infrastructure or passenger services. Contraction of freight facilities continued, but redundant trackbed and structures remained largely intact as stubborn reminders of Victorian engineering. Changes became more noticeable and gathered pace in the 1980s so that by the end of this decade certain parts of Nottingham's once extensive railway system were unrecognisable. Derelict railway land was sold off and new roads, housing and trading estates obliterated many once familiar sites. Local authorities became increasingly involved with new railway projects, whilst the introduction of new passenger stock on a variety of new cross-country trains gave Nottingham's passengers a completely different travelling experience.

The loss of the Great Central and Great Northern in Nottingham

Freight traffic has traditionally kept the last remnants of a station or line alive before complete closure and demolition, and this was true of the former GC and GN through Nottingham.

As Victoria station was being demolished freight continued through the site to Colwick yard until 26 May 1968. Colwick struggled on a little longer dealing with coal traffic from Gedling and Cotgrave collieries until it too closed on 12 April 1970. For five years after the passage of the last passenger train freight to the MOD depot at Ruddington kept the former GC south of Nottingham open, trains running into the Victoria Street tunnel at Weekday Cross before reversing up the ex-GN line to Trent Lane Junction and reversing again on to ex-MR lines. Then a new connection with the Midland main line was brought into use at Loughborough at the beginning of April 1974 allowing Ruddington to be reached from the south and, barely a year later, during redevelopment of a large area of the Meadows in Nottingham, the ex-GC viaduct there and Arkwright Street station were demolished.

Gradually more of the former GC route through Nottingham and the ex-GN's connections with it began to disappear. At the end of February 1975 the final remains of the ex-GC's Queen's Drive goods depot closed, having been used since 1967 as coal wharves. At the beginning of 1978 the bridge across London Road, once part of the GN's High Level station there, was removed, and a little further to the east the steel trestle viaduct that once straddled the gas works sidings was taken apart. In May 1980 work began on dismantling the lattice bridges across Nottingham Midland station and, six years later, the GC's impressive four-track bridge across the Trent was cut up and its brick-lined steel piers crudely demolished with ball and chain. Bulwell viaduct came down at the beginning of 1989, and now new housing estates have encroached on most of the former GC and GN trackbeds north of Nottingham. Bits of blue brick viaduct remain in the city, some earmarked for possible light railway use, but it is questionable how long others will last.

Declining freight

In 1974 the furnaces at Stanton ironworks were blown out for the last time and, although BR continued to carry pipes away from the works,

by 1980 it was no longer carrying any iron ore, limestone or coke in the LMR's Nottingham Division. Revenue from freight then relied almost totally on the transport of coal, approximately 16 million tonnes per annum, which accounted for 80% of all freight business within the Division. The string of electricity generating power stations along the Trent kept the Nottingham pits and BR busy during this period but, following the miners' strike of 1985, a significant number of local collieries closed. On the ex-MR Leen Valley line, Hucknall shut on 31 October 1986 followed by Newstead and Linby in 1987, the latter after 76% of UDM members had voted in favour of redundancy payments or work at other pits. Production continued at Cotgrave, but the workforce was halved in 1989 and annual output immediately dropped to below one million tonnes for the first time in 20 years. Further north the colliery at Blidworth closed completely in 1989. At Gedling the workforce was halved between 1988 and 1990 from just over 1,200 to 616 miners, the pit closing altogether in November 1991. When recent government plans to shut more collieries are implemented, Nottinghamshire mining communities and BR Railfreight will suffer still further.

Toton yard is already a ghost of its former self. In the mid-1980s, despite 'Merry-go-round' trains, it still handled significant quantities of coal, though by then it no longer hump-shunted thousands of loose-coupled unfitted wagons. It also dealt with over 100 trains a week as a centre of the Speedlink network, trains being made up there for York, Westbury, Tinsley, Sheerness Junction, Willesden, Whitemoor and Warrington, with in-coming workings from Bescot, Hull and Dover. But this level of activity has not been maintained due both to the cutback in locally

mined coal and the abandonment in 1991 of Speedlink and the wagon load freight network. The number of sidings in the yard has already been reduced but further rationalisation seems inevitable if traffic to and from the Channel Tunnel cannot be attracted there.

The only other 'heavy' mineral handled locally is oil, the two-track terminal next to Rectory Junction on the Nottingham-Grantham line being the only remnant of Colwick yard.

Facilities for handling other local freight have also visibly contracted. In the mid-1970s when I used to travel regularly between Leicester and Nottingham, apart from industrial units being built on the site of the MPD, most of the yards and sidings along the line from Trent to Nottingham were still intact. Today the route is lined with very new buildings, with others being erected. The Central Ordnance Depot at Chilwell is no longer rail connected, and the site of the Beeston Boiler Co has recently been covered by a new housing estate. On the other side of the line, Boots chemical and pharmaceutical works has lost its sidings having donated the track to the Midland Railway Centre at Butterley in 1990. Opposite the Boots factory, Freightliners Ltd closed its Beeston (Nottingham) depot (along with Aberdeen, Dundee, Edinburgh, Newcastle, Longsight Manchester and Swansea) on 6 April 1987, and the yard is now used by the S&T Department. Tracks no longer diverge from Lenton South Junction to serve Wilford power station and Clifton Colliery — this site now being occupied by 'Toys-R-Us'. Between Mansfield Junction and Wilford Road all the sidings and railway buildings have been cleared away — the remains of the ex-MR Bonded Warehouse as recently as mid-October 1992 — and new offices for the Inland Revenue are being constructed on the site. Between Wilford Road and Carrington Street, close to the site of the MR's 1851 seven-storey grain warehouse, Nottinghamshire County Council's purpose-built Archive Office has just opened (March 1993) and, adjacent to this building, where the MR's huge 1896 goods and grain warehouse once stood (latterly National Carriers), the city's new Magistrates' Courts and Bridewell are under construction.

Further east the Colwick industrial estate — created after World War 1 with its own railway system, where during the 1959-60 'campaign' 15,102 wagons of sugarbeet arrived at British Sugar Corporation's Colwick factory from numerous local stations, as well as from the south of England — is no longer connected to the ex-GN Grantham line at Colwick East Junction. And the site of Colwick yard itself is now partially covered by a new retail park, the sale of bedding and carpets having replaced the stabling of 'B1s' and 'K2s'. Today almost all of Nottingham's freight goes by road, the completion of the M1 at the end of the 1960s having accelerated the transfer from rail to road.

The only significant railfreight survival, if it can be called that, is parcels traffic. In 1986 platform No 6 at Nottingham was resignalled so that this traffic and football specials could be dealt with there. This allowed the former AN&B&EJR's terminus on London Road — used as Nottingham's main parcels depot since the late 1960s — to be abandoned by BR, but not until £95,000 had been spent on restoring and cleaning the Grade 2 listed station buildings. At the time of writing, the station is undergoing yet another refurbishment for its proposed new use as Nottingham's industrial museum. As an aside, the ex-GN's London Road (High Level) station nearby had an equally large sum lav-ished upon it at the end of 1986 in the process of turning it into, as it turned out, a short-lived bar and restaurant.

Passenger services

The aftermath of Beeching's statistical modernisation and standardisation left BR's passenger timetables looking very simple when compared to those of 10 years before. But only a few years after Mansfield had lost its passenger services and all stations along the Erewash Valley had closed, statistics were brought into operation again, this time to justify the reopening of a station on the site of the former one at Alfreton. The first suggestions appeared in *Modern Railways* for June 1970 and, by the end of 1972, it was announced that 11 local authorities had agreed to contribute £35,000 towards the cost of a new station with large car park and connecting bus services to serve the towns of Mansfield, Kirkby-in-Ashfield and Sutton-in-Ashfield. Christened 'Alfreton & Mansfield Parkway' the new station opened on 7 May 1973 at the beginning of the new timetable when most main line expresses were booked to stop there.

At the same time, InterCity trains between Derby and St Pancras started calling at Long Eaton (formerly Sawley Junction), which had recently been provided with a car park for city commuters. Co-operation between the East Midlands Tourist Board and the LMR Nottingham Division led to the joint promotion of the Manchester-Harwich boat train, rerouted through Nottingham in the 1973 timetable changes, and the successful introduction of 'Ranger' tickets giving a week's unrestricted travel within the East Midlands. But the pattern of passenger services through Nottingham remained basically very simple, with trains con-

Left:
Thanks to a John Player Railway Club and British Rail joint venture, steam returned to Nottingham on 15 September 1987. BR Standard Class 4 4-6-0 No 75069 is seen here at platform No 6 next to a London-bound HST.
Nottingham Evening Post

Left:
One of the first generation of 'Sprinters', Class 150 No 150107, pulls away from platform No 4 at 10.45 with the Coventry-Lincoln service on 26 May 1992.
Author

Below left:
One of the new Class 158 units departing from Nottingham at 15.15 on 26 May 1992 passing the 13.30 from St Pancras arriving seven minutes late.
Author

centrated on the St Pancras-Sheffield, Crewe-Stoke-on-Trent-Derby-Lincoln, and Nottingham-Grantham routes.

In 1975 of the 16 weekday through trains between Nottingham and London, with an extra service on Fridays, only four took less then two hours to reach the capital, the others taking between 2hr 1min and 2hr 42min. In the opposite direction there were the same number of trains, five taking less then two hours to reach Nottingham from St Pancras.

Between Nottingham and Derby during the week there were basically 23 local trains with 21 in the opposite direction (a number being Lincoln-Newark-Crewe through workings), supplemented by a few Saturdays only services, a journey between the two cities stopping at all stations taking between 32 and 40min. Between Nottingham and Grantham the service consisted of 13 weekday trains each way, (with a few through trains to Skegness) and three on Sundays supplemented by an extra three each way during the summer months. Most journeys to Grantham took 44min with returns slightly faster at only 41min.

Apart from the curtailment of through trains from St Pancras to Glasgow, this remained the pattern into the early 1980s and, although Nottingham station had been cleaned externally, considerably enhancing the façade, and £300,000 spent on a new booking office and travel centre which opened in the summer of 1982, the services along the Midland main line had fallen behind those offered on other Inter-City routes. High Speed Trains had successfully replaced 'Deltics' on the East Coast main line but, at the beginning of 1981, *A Strategy for the Midland Line* published by the LMR Nottingham Division, backed by Nottinghamshire, Leicestershire, Derbyshire and Northamptonshire County Councils reiterated the view that only electrification and introduction of the Advanced Passenger Train could improve the services on the Midland route. In the report it was calculated that HSTs could give only a 1hr 41min journey time between Nottingham and St Pancras, whereas the APT could achieve a time of 1hr 25min. But electrification would have to follow resignalling south of Loughborough, and it was estimated that at best the improvements would not be realised until 1990.

Despite these predictions, when it became obvious that Government investment would not be forthcoming for electrification, BR decided to introduce HST sets between St Pancras and Sheffield, which they did between October 1982 and May 1983. Services were completely revolutionised. Of the 14 London-Nottingham HST runs daily Monday-Friday, only one, the 07.00 ex-St Pancras, took longer than two hours — by just one minute — and four — the 11.30, 14.15, 17.25 and 20.40 ex-St Pancras — were booked to cover the distance in just 1hr 39min, psychologically faster than the 1981 report's projected timing. Another four took between 1hr 43min and 1hr 48min, and five just under the two hour barrier. In the opposite direction the 15 HST workings were generally not as fast, only one achieving a journey time of 1hr 39min (the 14.27 ex-Nottingham), but, nevertheless, 10 covered the ground in a creditable 12-18min under two hours, and only the 15.50 ex-Nottingham was booked to take exactly two hours between the cities. It was the boost the line needed, and when, in 1983, the Divisional Manager of the Nottingham Division reported that the number of journeys between Nottingham and London had increased by 35% compared with 1981, and revenue by 31%, the investment appeared fully justified.

Travelling north from Nottingham, however, the service was not as impressive, and appeared to be of more interest to the enthusiast than the ordinary passenger. In May 1982 trains between Nottingham and Glasgow had been routed away from the former MR's Leeds, Settle & Carlisle line, to the West Coast main line via Manchester and Preston. When the HSTs began to operate over the Midland route they offered seven journeys of 48min duration each way between Nottingham and Sheffield during the week. The additional five locomotive-hauled trains between these cities consisted of three which provided through services to and from Manchester Victoria as well, (one to and from Barrow-in-Furness, and two to and from Glasgow). By the fastest of these trains Nottingham was 2hr 24min away from Manchester, and Manchester 2hr 18min from Nottingham, the 10.44 from Nottingham and the returning 15.06 from Manchester being named *The European*. But,

excepting summer Saturday specials, travelling either north or south, all other long distance destinations from Nottingham had to be achieved by changing trains.

This lack of adequate cross-country services made the next revolution in travel from Nottingham all the more impressive, although there were problems and its effect of producing overcrowded trains has yet to be solved and may dim the obvious technical and timetabling achievements. At the beginning of January 1982 BR was divided into business 'sectors', most local and cross-country services becoming the responsibility of the Provincial Sector. At first there was nothing to show for this management change but, at the beginning of 1986, the first of the new Class 150 two-coach 'Sprinter' units began to operate through Nottingham. On 20 January that year the new units were officially launched at Nottingham station with local athletes racing along platform No 3 and local dignitaries delivering the obligatory speeches. With the introduction of the May 1986 timetable Sprinters from Lincoln began to work through to Birmingham New Street via Nottingham and, as an example of the service improvement, five minutes was clipped off a typical journey between Nottingham and Newark. Concurrently, trains from Crewe no longer ran through to Lincoln but either terminated at Nottingham or went forward to Grantham. In the same timetable changes, Nottingham found itself in direct contact with Leeds for the first time in years when six through weekday trains, with five return journeys Monday to Friday, an extra Fridays only and four on Saturdays were introduced. These trains also served a new station at Langley Mill, reopened on 12 May for £130,000. Of this sum 60% was raised by Derbyshire County Council, 20% from Nottinghamshire County Council, 15% from Amber Valley District Council and the rest from other local parish councils.

From then on, after years of stagnation the local timetable began to change every year as the services became more adventurous with the introduction of new stock, and something of the old GC's flair for publicity and marketing began to reappear. In the summer of 1987 Nottingham station underwent a welcomed repaint, and by the end of the year Roger Ford commented in *Modern Railways* that 'everything was falling into place for BR's Provincial Sector. For the first time in decades, there was a coherent commercial vision for BR's cross-country services between major conurbations.' On 16 May 1988 the Sheriff of Nottingham, J. Maddocks, was invited to wave off a new Class 156 'Super-Sprinter' forming the 11.27 Nottingham-Cam-

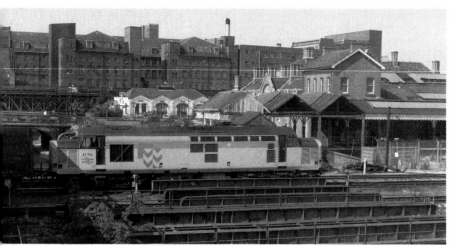

bridge 'Express', one of 15 weekday trains between Nottingham and Manchester, with 14 return workings. The new service comprised seven through Norwich-Liverpool trains each way, and a number of through Ipswich-Blackpool, Cambridge-Blackpool, Ely-Liverpool and Harwich-Manchester trains, all serving Peterborough. Travelling on these trains meant that Nottingham was only an hour from Peterborough, and just over an hour and three quarters away from Cambridge or Manchester compared with a previous time of 2hr 15min. Unfortunately, a casualty of these alterations was the through Nottingham-Leeds service, which, after only two years of operation, was cut from a basic six weekday trains each way to one token return journey.

The next step in the revolution faltered slightly, delayed by the late delivery of the new Class 158 units. The contract had been awarded to BREL in November 1987, but it was not until September 1990 that the first units entered service. In the meantime trains were cancelled, overcrowding was exacerbated and the resulting public criticism was not good for business. Undaunted, Provincial, recently renamed 'Regional Railways', started up its publicity machine, and a series of competitions, radio interviews, and press coverage culminated in a host of photocalls throughout the Midlands at the end of April and the beginning of May 1991 prior to the introduction of the summer timetable and the new stock. But behind the 'hype' there was truly a product to be proud of, and when the new timetable appeared, the number of trains between Nottingham and Manchester had been increased to 18, made up of six through services between Stansted Airport and Liverpool via Cambridge and Peterborough, with five return workings, plus a number of trains

originating from and terminating at Cambridge, Ely, Harwich, Great Yarmouth and Norwich.

Another, almost incidental, result of introducing these cross-country trains, was the acceleration of the traditional local services. For example, the fastest Regional Railways train between Nottingham and Derby can now complete the journey in just 18min, and even stopping at all stations the best time is only 28min. Between Nottingham and Grantham the fastest journey takes 34min compared to an all stations service of 45min. A typical all stations journey between Nottingham and Newark takes 33min but, with the welcome return of the occasional non-stop service, the trip can be achieved in just 22min.

InterCity services to and from Nottingham are also currently performing well after a low in 1987 when the best service between St Pancras and Nottingham had slipped to 1hr 43 min. Today (1993), during the week the fastest train is the 'Robin Hood', the 09.09 Nottingham Pullman service taking 1hr 34 min to St Pancras, returning from the capital at 18.59 and reaching Nottingham 1hr 31 min later. Of the other 15 up and 17 down trains Monday-Friday, five in each direction are also booked to complete their journeys in less than 1hr 40min. At weekends the 'Robin Hood' does not run, and on Saturdays there are 10 Nottingham-St Pancras trains with 12 in the opposite direction, of which only two each way take less than 1hr 40min. On Sundays the nine up and 10 down journeys are significantly slower.

Services north of Nottingham are now dominated by 'Sprinters' and Class 158 units, there being only two HSTs to Sheffield via Nottingham Monday-Saturdays with one on Sundays, and two in the opposite direction Mondays-Fridays with one on Saturdays and Sundays. With no regular locomotive-hauled passenger trains through Nottingham now, the contrast between accommodation on InterCity and Regional Railways services is very noticeable. With limited resources, Regional Railways has obviously pinned its hopes on more frequent and speedy services. But one great advantage of rail travel over the private car for the business man is the ability to work on the train between departure and destination. This is almost impossible on a 'Sprinter', and none of the new multiple-units have first-class accommodation. As Regional Railways publicity and marketing encourages more people to use these services, relying almost wholly on two-coach operation, and if travelling out to Newark or Lincoln very often on one-coach Class 153 units, with no spare stock available, this and overcrowding could take much of the shine off an otherwise very impressive revolution in local and cross-country services through Nottingham.

New lines and stations

The 1980s also witnessed not only the introduction of new stock and more adventurous timetabling, but the first co-ordinated attempt to expand the local passenger network for over 90 years. Currently there are two Nottinghamshire County Council sponsored projects being developed. One is the 'Greater Nottingham Light Rapid Transit' system with the aim of establishing a tram link between Nottingham Midland station, the city centre, Basford, Babbington and Hucknall. Part of this scheme relies on the second project, a joint NCC and Regional Railways 'heavy rail' initiative to reintroduce trains between Nottingham, Mansfield and Worksop over the ex-MR Leen Valley line, now christened the 'Robin Hood Line'. This will involve the reinstatement of the line between Newstead and Mansfield which has been physically removed. It is proposed that both trains and trams should use the route between Basford and Hucknall.

Following a study carried out in the mid-1980s, support for the 'Robin Hood Line' was forthcoming from other local authorities, for example Derbyshire County Council and Mansfield District Council, and the bill went before Parliament in 1989. The initial move towards achieving the reopening was to reprieve the threatened Radford Junction-Trowell Junction line, which also became the route for the new 'Super-Sprinter' and 158 services. Financial backing from NCC for the 'Robin Hood Line' was formally approved on 2 July 1991 — (£6 million), but unfortunately this was not matched by Government money. Nevertheless, work began on Phase 1 (Radford Junction, Bestwood Park

Junction to Newstead) during the summer of 1992.

On May 8 1993, Regional Railways were able to hold a 'Fun Day' to promote the new service between Nottingham and Newstead, and from 17 May when 15 passenger trains each way began to use the line, a simple platform put Newstead back on the railway map, and at Hucknall the road overbridge once again gave access to a single platform, the trackbed of the old up line and colliery sidings providing the site for a large adjacent car park. The trains became so popular, that within weeks of the reopening three-car DMUs had to be brought in to replace overcrowded Class 156 'Super-Sprinters' on Saturdays and during the schools' half-term. It is hoped to reopen a station at Bulwell in February 1994 and, as Government money has now been secured, it is optimistically hoped to reopen to Mansfield by May 1995 and to Worksop by late 1996.

But this is only the beginning as far as Regional Railways is concerned. Concurrently there are plans to reopen stations at Ilkeston, Trowell, Sandiacre, Long Eaton (Central), and Gedling as well as adding completely new stations at Woolaton, Radcliffe (Park & Ride), Cotgrave, and Saxondale (Park & Ride). Interestingly Lenton appears on the proposals, the first station within the city boundaries to have closed back in 1911 because of tram competition, and both Attenborough and Burton Joyce are targeted as sites for new Park & Ride stations.

The most ambitious local Regional Railways project for the next century — only seven years away — is to link the Cotgrave Colliery branch with the former MR's Nottingham-Melton Mowbray line just north of Stanton tunnel south of Normanton-on-the-Wolds in order to offer '...a more direct link to the South East...'. If this is indeed a viable project, then not only does the decision to abandon the original Nottingham-Melton Mowbray line in the 1960s become questionable, but so too does the comparatively recent loss of the route through West Bridgford which might finally have benefited from a station, and the conversion of the railway bridge over the Trent at Nottingham for road use.

Regional Railways in Nottingham

Most of what has been achieved, and what remains to be done, is the responsibility of Regional Railways Central, East Midlands and Lincolnshire District, based in 'Forward House', the former MR parcels office, Station Street, Nottingham. Adopting the motto of the former

GC, Regional Railways District Office moved there in 1991 and currently has a management and administrative staff of 80. With responsibility for sponsoring services in an area enclosed by Doncaster, Sheffield, Crewe, Stafford, Birmingham, Coventry, Leicester, Peterborough, Skegness and Grimsby, there are seven departments at Nottingham: Operations, Civil Engineering & PW, Retail, Finance, Personnel, S & T, and Premises Management, as well as the District's Control Office. Regular contact between other business sectors takes place approximately every month in Route and Business negotiating groups, with other working groups such as Operations meeting to discuss day-to-day issues. In April 1992 the 'Regions' of BR disappeared, and now the station at Nottingham is wholly the responsibility of Regional Railways, with the travel centre leased to InterCity and the two buffets rented out to Travellers Fare. Trent power box is owned by InterCity but the majority of its running costs are now financed by Regional Railways.

Regional Railways' income is generated from passenger receipts, property sales and central government funding via the PSO for the maintenance of existing services. Any new projects have to be self-financing in the first year before they become eligible for PSO money, and therefore NCC money is used to 'pump-prime'. Regular meetings are held with both members and officers of the local authorities, and new initiatives come from both them and Regional Railways in Nottingham. Computer models are now used to assess new projects, and with schemes like the reopening of the Leen Valley ('Robin Hood') line, and plans to reopen most of the local stations on the Erewash Valley line emerging as a result, it seems a great pity such models were not available for those who put the Beeching Report together.

Compared to the resources of the MR at Nottingham, Regional Railways Central, East Midlands & Lincolnshire District is a very small scale operation. Exactly one hundred years ago, the MR was planning to spend £18,787 building an oil gas works at Nottingham and convert 429 carriages to burn this gas for lighting. Today's facilities are tailored to suit very different operating environments. On the site of the former Eastcroft carriage sidings there are facilities for carriage washing, refuelling, general maintenance and overnight stabling, the latter being also provided at Lincoln, Boston and, until the end of March 1993, at Derby. The equipment all looks somewhat flimsy compared with the massively engineered cast and wrought-iron, blue-brick and terracotta, and even the generous proportions of wood used by Nottingham's previous building contractors and railway engineers. But, considering the depth of the current recession, and witnessing the relentless closure of the country's collieries and with them a considerable loss of revenue for BR, it is heartening that Regional Railways in Nottingham is visibly making improvements to passenger services and in partnership with local authorities investing in the latest equipment that might one day help to relieve road congestion, and win more 'customers' back to the city's railways.

Left:
At 12.09 on 6 March 1993, No 60013 *Robert Boyle* **heads eastwards along the ex-MR line to Lincoln past the ex-GN signalbox that once controlled the yard at London Road (Low Level) station seen in the background. To the left is the site of the Eastcroft carriage sidings.** *Author*

Appendix 1: MR trains between Nottingham and London 1842-1922

1842

London Euston	Nottingham	Nottingham	London Euston
6am	12.10pm (6hr 10min)	8.15am	3.15pm (7hr)
9.15am	3.15pm (6hr)	10.40am	6pm (7hr 20min)
11am	5.30pm (6hr 30min)	1.15pm	7.45pm (6hr 30min)
5pm	10.50pm (5hr 50min)	4.40pm	11.15pm (6hr 35min)
9pm	4.10am (7hr 10min)	9pm	5am (8hr)

1852

London Euston	Nottingham	Nottingham	London Euston
9am (?)	2.55pm (5hr 55min)	6am	11am (5hr)
6am	10am (4hr)	8.10am	?
6.30am	12.5pm (5hr 35min)	11am	6.20pm (7hr 20min)
9.15am	12.40pm (3hr 25min)	12.30pm	4.15pm (3hr 45min)
10.30am	3.30pm (5hr)	2pm	7.30pm (5hr 30min)
7pm	4.30am (9hr 30min)	4.10pm	9.45pm (5hr 35min)
12 midnight	6.23am (6hr 23min)	5.35am	10am (4hr 25min)
4am	9.10am (5hr 10min)	10pm	4.30am (6hr 30min)

1862

London King's X	Nottingham	Nottingham	London King's X
7.20am	12.55pm (5hr 35min)	6am	10.5am (4hr 5min)
9.10am	12.15pm (3hr 5min)	8.5am	1.40pm (5hr 35min)
9.20am	1.10pm (3hr 50min)	12.20pm	3.40pm (3hr 20min)
11.30am	3.5pm (3hr 35min)	3.5pm	6.10pm (3hr 5min)
5.35pm	8.35pm (3hr)	6.20pm	10pm (3hr 40min)
6.45pm	1.10am (6hr 25min)		

1872

London St Pancras	Nottingham	Nottingham	London St Pancras
6.15am	10.5am (3hr 50min)	5.25am (mail)	9.40am (4hr 15min)
8.30am	12.3pm (3hr 33min)	8.40am	12 noon (3hr 20min)
10am	1.8pm (3hr 8min)	11.35am	2.47pm (3hr 12min)
11.45am	3.25pm (3hr 40min)	12.35pm	4.10pm (3hr 35min)
3pm	6.30pm (3hr 30min)	3.15pm	6.40pm (3hr 25min)
5pm	8.9pm (3hr 9min)	5.15pm	8.35pm (3hr 20min)
5.30pm	9.40pm (4hr 10min)	6.40pm	9.52pm (3hr 12min)
8.35pm (mail)	12.15am (3hr 40min)	7.45pm	11.35pm (3hr 50min)
		12.30am (mail)	4.15am (3hr 45min)

1882

London St Pancras	Nottingham	Nottingham	London St Pancras
5.15am	8.3am (2hr 48min)	4.50am*	7.55am (3hr 5min)
8.10am	12.30pm (4hr 20min)	6.13am (mail)	10.30am (4hr 17min)
10am	12.35pm (2hr 35min)	10.15am	12.55pm (2hr 40min)
10.35am*	1.30pm (2hr 55min)	12.30pm	3.10pm (2hr 40min)
12.15pm	2.55pm (2hr 40min)	12.32pm	6.43pm (6hr 11min)
3.00pm	5.40pm (2hr 40min)	3.20pm	6pm (2hr 40min)
5.30pm	8.10pm (2hr 40min)	3.43pm	7.20pm (3hr 37min)
9.15pm*	12.25am (3hr 10min)	5.10pm	7.50pm (2hr 40min)
12.01am	3.15am (3hr 14min)	5.35pm	8.40pm (3hr 5min)
		7.20pm	10pm (2hr 40m)
		9.18pm	2.15am (4hr 57min)
		12.50am (mail)	4.15am (3hr 25min)

* 'Scotch Express'

1892

London St Pancras	Nottingham	Nottingham	London St Pancras
5.15am	8.3am (2hr 48min)	4.30am (MO)	8.20am (3hr 50min)
9am	11.33am (2hr 33min)	5.15am (MX)	8.20am (3hr 5min)
10am	12.45pm (2hr 45min)	5.55am	10.30am (4hr 35min)
10.35am	1pm (2hr 25min)	8.30am	11.10am (2hr 40min)
12.25pm	2.57pm (2hr 32min)	10.20am	12.55pm (2hr 35min)
2pm	4.50pm (2hr 50min)	11.10am	2.50pm (3hr 40min)

London St Pancras	Nottingham		Nottingham	London St Pancras
3pm	5.30pm (2hr 30min)		12.45pm	3.20pm (2hr 35min)
4pm	7.20pm (3hr 20min)		3.27pm	6.5pm (2hr 38min)
5.40pm	8.10pm (2hr 30min)		5.35pm	8.5pm (2hr 30min)
9.15pm	12.30am (3hr 15min)		7.42pm	10.20pm (2hr 38min)
12 midnight	3.15am (3hr 15min)		12.50am	4.15am (3hr 25min)

1902

London St Pancras	Nottingham		Nottingham	London St Pancras
5.15am	8am (2hr 45min)		4.35am (MO)	7.35am (3hr)
8.30am	11am (2hr 30min)		5.22am (MX)	7.50am (2hr 28min)
9.35am	11.56am (2hr 21min)		5.25am (MX)	8.5am (2hr 40min)
10.30am	12.53pm (2hr 23min)		5.55am	10.30am (4hr 35min)
12.15pm	2.41pm (2hr 26min)		6.48am (SX)	9.50am (3hr 2min)
1.30pm	4.16pm (2hr 46min)		7.25am	10.55am (3hr 30min)
2.10pm	4.33pm (2hr 23min)		8.33am	11.10am (2hr 37min)
3pm	5.32pm (2hr 32min)		10.35am	1pm (2hr 25min)
4.5pm	7.00pm (2hr 55min)		11.15am	2.10pm (2hr 55min)
5pm	7.24pm (2hr 24min)		1.10pm	3.40pm (2hr 30min)
5.40pm	8.5pm (2hr 25min)		2.36pm	5pm (2hr 24min)
6.45pm	9.38pm (2hr 53min)		3.25pm	6.10pm (2hr 45min)
7.15pm	10.8pm (2hr 53min)		5.6pm	7.35pm (2hr 29min)
9.15pm	11.43pm (2hr 28min)		5.30pm	7.50pm (2hr 20min)
12.15am	3.30am (3hr 15min)		7pm	10pm (3hr)
			8.10pm	10.30pm (2hr 20min)
			12.45am	4.20am (3hr 35min)

1912

London St Pancras	Nottingham		Nottingham	London St Pancras
4.50am	7.48am (2hr 58min)		4.28am (MX)	7.35am (3hr 7min)
8am	10.40am (2hr 40min)		5.12am (MO)	7.35am (2hr 23min)
9.30am	12.17pm (2hr 47min)		5.10am (MX)	8.5am (2hr 55min)
10.25am	12.52pm (2hr 27min)		6.3am (MX)	8.15am (2hr 12min)
11.30am	2.15pm (2hr 45min)		5.32am (SO)	9.20am (3hr 48min)
12.7pm	2.25pm (2hr 18min)		6.35am (SX)	9.20am (2hr 45min)
2.5pm	4.35pm (2hr 30min)		8.25am	10.40am (2hr 15min)
3.30pm	5.45pm (2hr 15min)		8.30am	11.32am (3hr 2min)
4.55pm	7.18pm (2hr 23min)		9.25am	12.5pm (2hr 40min)
5.35pm (SX)	8.20pm (2hr 45min)		10.40am	1.15pm (2hr 35min)
6pm	8.30pm (2hr 30min)		11.28am (SX)	1.57pm (2hr 29min)
6.30pm	9.35pm (3hr 5min)		11.52am (Th/SX)	3pm (3hr 8min)
8.15pm (SX)	10.37pm (2hr 22min)		12.28pm	3.47pm (3hr 19min)
9.30pm	11.50pm (2hr 20min)		1.30pm	4pm (2hr 30min)
12 midnight	2.40am (2hr 40min)		3.3pm	5.25pm (2hr 22min)
			3.55pm	6.15pm (2hr 20min)
			5pm	7.42pm (2hr 42min)
			5.15pm	8.15pm (3hr)
			6.53pm	10pm (3hr 7min)
			7.42pm	10.25pm (2hr 43min)
			8.25pm	11.15pm (2hr 50min)
			12.45am	4.20am (3hr 35min)

1922

London St Pancras	Nottingham		Nottingham	London St Pancras
7.50am	11.5am (3hr 15min)		4.30am	7.25am (H) (2hr 55min)
9am	11.15am (A) (2hr 15min)		5.30am	8.3am (I) (2hr 33min)
11am	1.33pm(B) (2hr 33min)		7am	9.57am (2hr 57min)
1.50pm	4.5pm (C) (2hr 15min)		8.23am	10.45am (2hr 22min)
3.30pm	5.50pm (2hr 20min)		10.30am	1.20pm (J) (2hr 50min)
4.30pm	7.38pm (3hr 8min)		1.40pm	4.10pm (K) (2hr 30min)
5pm	7.15pm (D) (2hr 15min)		2.57pm	5.30pm (L) (2hr 33min)
5.40pm	8.34pm (2hr 54min)		4.50pm	7.10pm (M) (2hr 20min)
6.15pm	8.48pm (2hr 33min)		5.25pm	8.20pm (2hr 55min)
6.30pm	11.12pm (4hr 42min)		6.20pm	9.15pm (F) (2hr 55min)
9.15pm	11.42pm (E) (2hr 27min)		6.45pm	9.5pm (N) (2hr 20min)
9.30pm (SX)	11.58pm (F) (2hr 28min)		3.50am (MX)	6.00am (2hr 10min)
11.45pm	2.26am (G) (2hr 41min)			

Notes

A   'Scotch Express', arr Edinburgh 6.34pm
B   'Sheffield Express', arr 2.53pm
C   'Yorkshire Express', arr Bradford 6.45pm
D   'Belfast Boat Express', arr Leeds 9.25pm
E   sleeper to Edinburgh, arr 7.12am
F   'Scotch Express'
G   sleeper to Glasgow

H   'Scotch Express', sleeper from Glasgow
I   'Scotch Express', sleeper from Edinburgh
J   dep Leeds 8am
K   dep Bradford 10.25am
L   dep Leeds 1pm
M   'Scotch Express' with through carriage Glasgow-Nottingham
N   dep Sheffield 5.30pm

Appendix 2: Locomotive Allocations

Locomotives allocated to Nottingham LMS shed No 18, as at July 1933

Class	Type	Number
Kirtley '890' '1P'	2-4-0	87
Johnson 6ft 6in '1P'	2-4-0	162/83
Johnson 6ft 9in '1P'	2-4-0	245
Johnson 7ft unrebuilt '1P'	4-4-0	311
Johnson rebuilt & Fowler superheated '2P'	4-4-0	404-11/5-23/7/30/8
Johnson 'Belpaire' '3P'	4-4-0	721/6
Johnson '4P'	4-4-0	925-8
Fowler 'Compound' '4P'	4-4-0	1092-7
Johnson '1P'	0-4-4T	1249/52/97
Johnson '1P'	0-4-4T	1301-3/6/12/3/25/40-2/4/7/73/9
Johnson '2F' & '3F'	0-6-0	3227/39/49, 3319/20/4/7/32/59/67-72/4/7/8/81/2/3/5, 3458/9/94/6, 3510/1/4/7/8/48/71/2/4/7/8/83-7/90/2/8, 3613/33/4/6/7
Johnson/Deeley '3F'	0-6-0	3759/60/2/4-7, 3811/45/6/ 94/5/6
Fowler '4F'	0-6-0	3948/54-9, 4035/40/53-6/82, 4100/96, 4202/4/5/6/64-8, 4401/12-6, 4547
Webb '1F'	0-4-2ST	6400/1
Webb 'Watford' tank '2P'	0-6-2T	6906
Fowler '3F'	0-6-0T	7118/9, 16537/8, 16632-5, 16715
Hughes/Fowler '5P/4F'	2-6-0	13051, 13123-7/49

Locomotives allocated to Toton shed No 17, as at July 1933

Class	Type	Number
Deeley '0F'	0-4-0T	1531
Johnson '1F'	0-6-0T	1856
Deeley '3P'	0-6-4T	2017
Kirtley '1F'	0-6-0	2835
Johnson '2F' & '3F'	0-6-0	2920/46/72/83/7/90/3, 3011/24/44/5/90, 3131/4/51, 3220/32, 3304, 3466/99, 3500/3, 3719/45/78/80/7/93-5/8/9, 3803/4/5/10/6-21/3-8/31-4
Fowler '4F'	0-6-0	3901/22/3/69-76/9, 4011-5, 4102/32, 4227/74/5/9
Beyer-Garratt	2-6-0-0-6-2T	4967-83/5/6/98/9
Fowler '3F'	0-6-0T	7117-9, 16526/9-33, 16716-8
Webb '2F'	0-6-2T	7858
Fowler '7F'	0-8-0	9553-5/96-9

Locomotives noted at Colwick LNER shed, as at May 1936

Class	Type	Number
Robinson 'B8'	4-6-0	5004 *Glenalmond*, 5439 *Sutton Nelthorpe*
Ivatt 'C12'	4-4-2T	4506/13/5/6/23/6/48
Ivatt 'D2'	4-4-0	3047/8/50, 4322/6/7/9/62-5/71/91/3
Ivatt 'D3'	4-4-0	3400, 4301/6/10/2/8/41/5/6/52/3
Robinson 'D9'	4-6-0	6025/35/7-9
Ivatt 'J2'	0-6-0	3076-8
Ivatt 'J3' & 'J4'	0-6-0	3177/9, 3332/50/75/90, 4033/5, 4092/4/6, 4109/11/41/3/62/71
Ivatt & Gresley 'J6'	0-6-0	3521/4/5/36/8/40-5/50-3/7/62-6/73/6/81/3/7, 3601/21/3/5/7-9
Robinson 'J11'	0-6-0	5223/34/42/97, 5308/13/22, 5991
Gresley 'J39'	0-6-0	1281, 1495, 2696, 2976
Ivatt 'J52', 'J53' & 'J55'	0-6-0ST	3918/9/65/6, 4055, 4203/6/8/10/40/59/60/4/8/73/6/83
Pollitt 'N5'	0-6-2T	5546, 5899, 5923
Robinson 'O4'	2-8-0	5001/8, 5382/3/5/7/99, 5405, 6192, 6204/7/11/8/25/46/64/70/9/95, 6308/11/22/4/36/8/61/3/8/77, 6497, 6505/9/10/21/8/30/40/1/5/65/73/86/7, 6600/1/6/19/24

Railcar No 43306

Locomotives allocated to Nottingham (16A), as at 1959

Class	Type	Number
'2P'	4-4-0	40041/21/54/87/93/502/4/34/42/50/57/85/632
'4'	2-6-4T	42140/61/85/636
'4F'	0-6-0	43856/9/88/917/8/28/54/8/62/72,
		44018/21/30/3/95/131/2/9/51/8/95/204/15/23/48/313/94/401/12/14/72/80/533/46/55/77/8/85
'5'	4-6-0	44806/58/61/918/44/, 45088/253/63
'Jubilee'	4-6-0	45611 *Hong Kong*, 45620 *North Borneo*, 45636 *Uganda*, 45641 *Sandwich*, 45650 *Blake*,
		45667 *Jellicoe*
'3F'	0-6-0T	47277
'8F'	2-8-0	48000/64/108/17/70/7/217/8/61/79/86/377/614/35/9/53/66/75/86/748/63
'2F'	0-6-0	58175
'4'	4-6-0	75056/62-4

Locomotives allocated to Toton (18A), as at 1959

Class	Type	Number
'3P'	4-4-2T	41947
'3F'	0-6-0	43251/309/453/99/650/793/826/31
'4F'	0-6-0	43845/60/5/921/90/4, 44012/106/40/61/78/200/24/84/376/427
'3F'	0-6-0T	47223/47/551
'8F'	2-8`0	48099/118/28/45/83-7/94-7/201/21/71/84/304/6/14/9/24/32/3/8/50/61-3/
		7/70/84/7/90/507/17/30/8/45/604/6/7/15/6/20/36/7/40/62/72/81/5/94/8/728
'2F'	0-6-0	58153/66/73
'9F'	2-10-0	92050/7/77/8/86/84/129-31/53/6/8

Locomotives allocated to Colwick (40E), as at 1959

Class	Type	Number
'4'	4-6-0	43154/5/8
'B1'	4-6-0	61088/92/141/63/77/85/8/209/81/99
'K2'	2-6-0	17623/38/52-4/80
'K3'	2-6-0	61808/21/33/7/52/70/3/88/96/914/47/74/82
'O1' & 'O4'	2-8-0	63585/7/9/92/4/602/14/39/47/57/74/5/94/9/754/68/70/816/59/63/73
'J6'	0-6-0	64213/35/8/9/57/69/73
'J11'	0-6-0	64348/97/438
'J39'	0-6-0	64712/5/35/62/3/802/32/87/974/6/7/80/3/8
'L1'	2-6-4T	67753/8/60/88/99
'J94'	0-6-0T	68028/72/6
'J69'	0-6-0T	68522/45/50/601/29
'J50'	0-6-0T	68893/927/50/67/74/5
'A5'	4-6-2T	69800/5/9/12/25
'WD'	2-8-0	90002/5/24/5/37/8/50/2/3/64/73/5/84/103/4/15/8/20/30/46/54/61/6/85/9/
		202/15/35/88/96/303/68/04/432/7/73/6/96/519/618/29/34/62/703/17
'9F'	2-10-0	92186

Locomotives allocated to Toton (TO), as at 1980

Class	Type	Number
'08'	0-6-0	018/21/7/45, 275/92/3, 320/30/2/4, 610/7/85, 741/57, 829/56/8/94
'20'	Bo-Bo	030/40-5/7/8/50/63/4/6-77/81/4/7/8/90/7, 113/34-6/9-43/7/8/50-78/80-3/
		5-90/2-9
'25'	Bo-Bo	073/4, 101/7/15/8/21-7/9-37/52, 212/4/48/9/54/7/8/64/7-70/9/80, 301-3/
		8-12/20/1
'44'	1Co-Co1	004/7/8
'45'	1Co-Co1	003-5/8/42/51/2/4-60/2/4-77, 101-50
'47'	Co-Co	204/81, 306/15/20-30/43/59/64/9
'56'	Co-Co	036/9/42/7-65 (class still being delivered)